Other books written by Dr. Tramontana

Hypnotically Enhanced Addictions Treatment: Alcohol Abuse, Drug Abuse, Gambling, Weight Loss, and Smoking Cessation. Crown House Publishing, 2009.

Sports Hypnosis in Practice: Scripts, Strategies, and Case Examples. Crown House Publishing, 2011.

GOLF

Peak Performance through
Self-Hypnosis Training

JOSEPH TRAMONTANA, PH.D.

ARCHWAY PUBLISHING

Copyright © 2021 Joseph Tramontana, Ph.D.

All rights reserved. No part of this book may be used or reproduced by any means, graphic, electronic, or mechanical, including photocopying, recording, taping or by any information storage retrieval system without the written permission of the author except in the case of brief quotations embodied in critical articles and reviews.

The information, ideas, and suggestions in this book are not intended as a substitute for professional advice. Before following any suggestions contained in this book, you should consult your personal physician or mental health professional. Neither the author nor the publisher shall be liable or responsible for any loss or damage allegedly arising as a consequence of your use or application of any information or suggestions in this book.

Archway Publishing books may be ordered through booksellers or by contacting:

Archway Publishing
1663 Liberty Drive
Bloomington, IN 47403
www.archwaypublishing.com
844-669-3957

Because of the dynamic nature of the Internet, any web addresses or links contained in this book may have changed since publication and may no longer be valid. The views expressed in this work are solely those of the author and do not necessarily reflect the views of the publisher, and the publisher hereby disclaims any responsibility for them.

Any people depicted in stock imagery provided by Getty Images are models, and such images are being used for illustrative purposes only. Certain stock imagery © Getty Images.

ISBN: 978-1-6657-0532-5 (sc)
ISBN: 978-1-6657-0533-2 (e)

Library of Congress Control Number: 2021906981

Print information available on the last page.

Archway Publishing rev. date: 04/26/2021

This book is dedicated to my children, Jim, a medical doctor, and Jody, a licensed clinical social worker, both of whom I am so proud, and their children, my grandchildren; in loving memory of my parents, Rosario and Theresa; and in loving memory of three of my sisters who have passed, Emily, Pam, and Terri, and the one who is still living, Susan. All four of my younger sisters were athletes in their own right; all could outrun any boy in the neighborhood—except for me, that is—and Susan is becoming quite a good golfer (from what she tells me).

I also dedicate this work to all my mentors in the hypnosis community.

CONTENTS

Preface ix
Acknowledgments xi
Introduction xiii

Chapter 1 Overview of Hypnotic and Self-Hypnotic
           Approaches in Sports 1
Chapter 2 Self-Hypnosis for Golfers 15
Chapter 3 Your Self-Hypnosis Training: Let's Begin 31
Chapter 4 Additional Techniques 49
Chapter 5 More on the Importance of Self-Hypnosis Practice ... 59
Chapter 6 General Hypnotic and Therapeutic Approaches ... 65
Chapter 7 Inspirational Stories and Affirmations 73
Chapter 8 Recovering from Injury and Returning to
           Training and Competition 77
Chapter 9 Anxiety Disorders 91
Chapter 10 Substance Abuse and Other Addictive Behaviors
           in Athletes 95

Conclusion 103
Appendix A 105
Appendix B 115
Appendix C 125
Closing Thoughts 133
References 135

PREFACE

My previous book on sports hypnosis was written for trained hypnotherapists and sports counselors working with athletes to improve their game. In that book, there is a chapter on working with golfers, the group with whom I have used these techniques the most by far, and I present a number of interesting case examples. Some of my clients asked if there was a book they could use to practice on their own in addition to the self-hypnosis I taught them to do in my office and instructed them to practice at home. This book is the culmination of those requests. To take the requests a step further, I wrote this book in a fashion that the golfer never has to work directly with a hypnotist, since most cities do not even have a hypnotherapist who works in the field of sports hypnosis.

I have been using hypnosis and hypnotherapy since 1978 for a wide variety of applications, including smoking cessation, weight-loss therapy, and other addictions, such as alcoholism and problematic drinking, drug abuse, and pathological gambling (Tramontana 2008, 2009). In addition, I also have had experience in successfully using hypnosis for pain control during surgical procedures (Tramontana 2008b), as well as in many other areas in which I have not published, including chronic pain, anxiety, obsessive-compulsive behaviors, fear of public speaking, trichotillomania, bedwetting, bruxism, and study habits and exam taking, among others.

In high school and college, I ran track, competing as a sprinter, and played football as a running back and linebacker, and in my later years, I became interested in endurance running. I ran a lot of 5Ks and 10Ks, a half dozen half-marathons, and three full marathons. Then I began coaching marathon runners and walkers for the Leukemia and Lymphoma Society's fundraising program called Team in Training.

To say that I love sports would be an understatement. I am a Saints season ticket holder, a Louisiana State University (my alma mater) fan, and a Pelicans fan.

ACKNOWLEDGMENTS

I owe thanks to a number of former athletes and coaches who assisted in my development of ideas and techniques for working with athletes in a number of sports. These individuals graciously agreed to be interviewed for my first book on sports hypnosis, *Sports Hypnosis in Practice: Scripts, Strategies, and Case Examples* (Tramontana 2011).

Brian Kinchen, a former National Football League tight end and long snapper as well as a pretty good amateur golfer, whose story I told in a condensed form in my previous book, gave me great insights into working with athletes in high-pressure competition. In addition, coaches Tony Minnis, formerly the coach of championship women's tennis teams at Louisiana State University (LSU); Yvette Girouard, an LSU women's softball coach who recently retired; and Leaf Boswell, coach of LSU's equestrian club team, were helpful in their openness and willingness to talk about the mental side of their respective sports. Golfers Greg Conley and Lisette Lee (now Prieto) and volleyball player Paige Huber-Pitts, former client athletes who agreed to be interviewed for that book, were all helpful. I enjoyed working with all of them, and it was great to hear from them years later how much the techniques I taught them proved helpful in their respective competitions. I've included in the case examples many other athletes with whom I have worked, but I do not mention them by name, for a number of reasons. Besides teaching them about the mental side of sports, I feel I have learned from all of them.

INTRODUCTION

> The greatest discovery of my generation is that a human being can alter his life by altering his attitude.
>
> —William James, nineteenth-century philosopher and psychologist

This book is geared toward the individual golfer. Therefore, there is a primary focus on self-hypnosis. The goal is to present techniques and methods you, the golfer, can employ just by reading the text. Of course, if you can work with a hypnotherapist who is experienced with sports hypnosis or who is familiar or becomes familiar with my book for therapists (*Sports Hypnosis in Practice: Strategies, Techniques, and Case Examples*), this approach will further reinforce the self-hypnosis work.

What Is Hypnosis?

While I did not feel the need to define hypnosis in my book geared toward experienced hypnotherapists, I will do so for those reading this work who are new to the field. While there are many definitions of hypnosis, the one I prefer is as follows:

> Hypnosis is a state of consciousness involving focused attention and reduced peripheral awareness characterized by an enhanced capacity for response to suggestion. (Elkins et al. 2015)

This is the definition now accepted by Division 30 (Clinical Hypnosis) of the American Psychological Association.

Many of you likely have misinformation about hypnosis, so as we get further into the book, I will spend some time telling you what it is and what it's not. A lot of the misinformation comes from stage hypnotists who try to convince their audiences they can use their mind power to control the audiences' minds. In clinical hypnosis, the idea is that I cannot control your mind, nor would I want to, but I can teach you to use your mind power to achieve your goals. This is even more evident in self-hypnosis training than in working with a hypnotherapist.

I am amused by the fact that some types of hypnosis or self-hypnosis must have been used back in the days of the Roman gladiators. I ask you to imagine someone entering an arena with a lion and contemplating his impending demise without at least being able to disassociate to some extent. I find it interesting that in those days, the emperors and the viewing public viewed that activity as sport. On the other hand, for the gladiators (athletes), it was a matter of life or death.

The psychology of sport is becoming an increasingly popular field of study and practice for psychologists. Coaches and sports counselors are also into these concepts, although they might use different terms (e.g., *visualization, relaxation, imagery,* and so on). I realized this phenomenon by attending meetings of the American Association of Sports Psychologists (AASP), which has more nonpsychologists (for example, coaches, sports counselors, and exercise physiologists) than psychologists as members. Other books worth reviewing are James Loehr's *The New Toughness Training in Sports* (1995), which has a foreword written by Chris Evert and Dan Jansen. Dr. Loehr has worked with many other famous athletes as well. In *Developing Sport Psychology within Your Clinical Practice* (1998), author Jack Lesyk includes a brief discussion on relaxation training, which he refers to as "a sort of light hypnosis" (65–66). William Morgan includes a chapter on hypnosis in sport and exercise psychology in *Exploring Sport and Exercise Psychology* (Van Raalte and Brewer 2002).

I joined the AASP to find out more about the focus of providers working with athletes without the use of hypnosis. At my first meeting of that organization in 2010, I had the opportunity to chat with Dr. Loehr. Dr. Loehr gave the keynote address at the AASP Annual Conference in Providence, Rhode Island (Loehr 2010). He was CEO and chairman of the Human Performance Institute in Orlando, Florida, where he works to enhance performance with athletes as well as corporations and military special forces. His techniques and strategies are similar across all these groups. He indicated to me that he had moved away from using hypnosis as a technique with athletes because he did not want them to feel he was the one in control of their improvement. However, once I explained to him that my focus was on training the athlete in self-hypnosis, his concern was negated.

Basically, the difference is this: I will be teaching you to use hypnotic techniques to achieve your goals. The emphasis is on your mind power, not mine, and your goals, not mine.

At the first AASP conference I attended, there were no presentations on hypnosis in sports included in the four days of lectures, symposia, and workshops, although I did hear a speaker make a perfunctory mention of hypnosis for relaxation. However, I found it interesting that the group, which included a cross section of psychologists, sports counselors, exercise physiologists, educators, and so on, talked about many of the same techniques I used, albeit with other names. The main difference was that they did not use formal hypnotic inductions or self-hypnotic training. Instead, they used terms such as *relaxation, concentration, mindfulness, focus, centering, visualization,* and *imagery,* all of which are a major focus of my approach. Many of the presentations dealt with mental skills training (MST) and goal setting, which to some extent incorporates the same techniques. My belief is that sports hypnosis is indeed a specialized form of sports psychology. As you will see in one of the case examples in chapter 2, the suggestions I give athletes are similar to those given by other sports counselors; the primary difference is that mine are given hypnotically rather than conversationally. I have found hypnotic and posthypnotic suggestions to be much more powerful than those given conversationally, and this has been reinforced by my clients.

A review in the American Psychological Association (APA) *Monitor on Psychology* (Schwartz 2008) shows psychologists are increasingly being called upon to help Olympians improve their concentration, focus their skills, and cope with the intense pressure of competition at such a high level. Schwartz reported on the responses of eleven psychologists she interviewed in the field. She described, for example, how Margaret Ottley, working with the US track-and-field team, reinforced the skills athletes already used, including breathing techniques, positive self-talk, and sensory awareness. Colleen Hacker, who worked with the US field hockey team, utilized performance-enhancement techniques such as imagery, focusing, distraction control, and preperformance routines. Schwartz indicated that aiding athletes in being their best more often and playing their best when it counted most were the goals of her work. Respondents in different events gave similar descriptions of their mental training of athletes.

In a 2008 American Society of Clinical Hypnosis (ASCH) newsletter, David Wark, former president of the ASCH, published an article titled "Report from the President's Desk." He talked about the First World Congress on Excellence in Sports and Life, which was held in Beijing, China, in August 2008. The conference brought together mental trainers from sports, business coaching, education, and health, and all of them were interested in the application of hypnosis as at least one aspect of mental training. It is obvious the popularity of this field is growing. (I was also pleased that Dr. Wark wrote a wonderful prepublication review of my prior sports hypnosis book.)

An article published in the *Wall Street Journal* made reference to the significance of people's beliefs and the mental models or mindsets that shape their behavior. The article reported that psychologists interviewed for the story believed people act and perform in accordance with the beliefs these models tell them are true. In other words, if people think something is not possible or out of their reach, they are probably not going to commit much energy or many resources to accomplishing that goal. Old habits die slowly, as the saying goes, because they are driven by outdated mindsets. Three steps are recommended in order to replace old habits through a change in your mindset. These suggestions reinforce what I've been teaching athletes for years.

1. You should begin by specifically identifying the results you want.
2. You must create and develop actions that will accomplish those results.
3. You should examine your beliefs about those actions to determine if they are holding you back.

In summary, if you want to achieve your goals, you must create a mindset made of beliefs that support the truth you desire in your future (see the last entry in the list of affirmations in appendix A, a poem titled "The Man Who Thinks He Can").

Dr. Tom Saunders is an interesting physician who merged his life's work with his life's pleasure: golf. When practicing medicine, he spent many years teaching self-hypnosis to patients. As a teacher, he inspired medical students to use the techniques to help their patients manage medical problems. After noticing the similarities between self-hypnosis and mental training programs for Olympians, he decided to try the techniques for his own golf game. After noticing improvement in his game, he began teaching the techniques to golfers and other athletes to help them reach their potential.

This experience by Dr. Saunders led to the 1996 publication of his book *Golf: The Mind-Body Connection: How to Lower Your Score with Mental Training*. His revised version, published in 2005, is titled *Golf: Lower Your Score with Mental Training*. The book refers primarily to mental training but has sections on hypnosis and self-hypnosis training. On the back cover of the book, he poses the following question: "Do you recognize yourself?"

He notes, "Your practice swing is smooth, relaxed and flowing ... swing like that and it will be a great shot ... but as you take the shot your muscles tighten, the swing speeds up and the fluidity drains away. The result is a real disappointment." He adds, summarizing the purpose of his book, "You can overcome this and many other problems by training your mind." This training helps you to focus completely on the shot you are about to make, develop positive thoughts and behavioral patterns, use mental imagery to improve your game, and achieve active relaxation.

There are a few other books that explicitly address sports hypnosis, including John Edgrette and Tim Rowan's *Winning the Mind Game* (2003) and Donald Liggett's *Sports Hypnosis* (2000).

Pratt and Korn (1996) gave an interesting interpretation in their response to questions regarding the efficacy of hypnosis in enhancing sports performance. The authors provided some basic information on how it might apply, including an example of how Ken Norton used self-hypnosis to prepare for the bout in which he beat Muhammad Ali. They noted that Norton was already a good boxer, so self-hypnosis did not suddenly transform him into a winner; rather, it helped him perform at his peak level.

I teach a class on hypnotherapy to advanced graduate students at the Chicago School of Professional Psychology's Xavier University of Louisiana in New Orleans campus, and I recently adopted *Trancework: An Introduction to the Practice of Clinical Hypnosis* by Michael D. Yapko (2012) as the textbook for the class. The lengthy book covers many aspects and applications of hypnosis, but he devotes only two paragraphs to sports hypnosis. Please note that this does not decrease the book's importance but only reflects that hypnosis is used much more for teaching patients and clients to cope with medical or psychological problems than to enhance peak performance. His words about sports hypnosis are significant nonetheless: "Engaging in athletics with any degree of intensity involves large measures of physical control and mental concentration."

Most golfers are interested in other sports, and many are familiar with the famous and usually comical quips of Yogi Berra, the quotable former baseball catcher and manager. For example, he said, "Nobody goes to that restaurant anymore, because it's too crowded." Yapko notes another famous Yogism: "Ninety percent of this game is half mental." While Yogi might have mangled the verbiage, Yapko says, the idea was sound.

Yapko notes that precise control over one's body is essential to giving an outstanding performance for an athlete. He says athletes often describe what they call "muscle memory," the keen awareness of how each limb and muscle must be positioned in order to perform successfully. Physical control through the amplification of the mind-body relationship can help athletes push their bodies to the upper limits of their talents (what I refer to as "peak performance").

As noted in the definition of *hypnosis* I mentioned above, hypnosis is a technique for narrowing one's attentional focus to the task at hand, which is a powerful tool to have available in sports.

Yapko notes that hypnosis is also important in managing the tension inherent in competition. Building positive expectations and positive communication with oneself can enhance performance dramatically. You will see in subsequent sections how I teach future projection or future-focused therapy to enable this phenomenon. These techniques are especially important for an athlete who is in a slump or troubled and likely having mental images of failure. For example, case number one in chapter 2 deals with a golfer who kept missing the cut on the last hole. I refer to this as "rehearsing failure" instead of "rehearsing success."

I describe my work with athletes as hypnotic coaching. I have had successful outcomes in working with athletes across many sports I have never played. One of my early experiences in the use of hypnosis occurred shortly after I attended a sports hypnosis workshop. A woman who knew I was doing some work in the area of hypnosis called me. She was coaching high school runners, and she asked if I could help with her own daughter, whom she did not coach. The girl was a high jumper. She said her daughter had been winning meets but then, for whatever reason, suddenly had begun hesitating right before the bar. I explained to the mother that I knew little about high-jumping but said perhaps she could ask her daughter's jumping coach to write down for me some of the key phrases she attempted to instill in her high jumpers. The suggestions were "Smooth, even approach," "Lift off your plant foot," "Arch your back," and "Tuck your butt," among others. I reinforced those statements hypnotically, with rapid and dramatic success. I saw the client on a Friday evening before a Saturday meet and made a recording of the session for her to listen to later that evening and the next morning. Not only did she not hesitate, but she jumped four inches higher than ever before. I was surprised, to say the least. My prior thinking had been that with the aid of self-hypnosis training, people could achieve at their best or peak level. By working with the high jumper, I realized that many athletes, especially younger ones, had not even yet achieved their peak level.

There are many books on sports psychology. As I said earlier, I see sports hypnosis as a subspecialty of sports psychology. Especially for golf, there are a number of source books, including Timothy Gallwey's *The Inner Game of Golf* (1981), Tom Saunders's *Lower Your Score through Mental Training* (2005), and several books by Robert Rotella, such as *Golf Is Not a Game of Perfect* (1995), *Golf Is a Game of Confidence* (1996), and *The Golfer's Mind* (2004). There are several others by Dr. Rotella listed in the recommended reading section.

Gallwey's book on golf was consistent with two he had previously published in other sports: *The Inner Game of Tennis* (1974) and *Inner Skiing* (1979). In his books, Gallwey shows how the mental aspects of a sport generalize across many sports. According to Gallwey, ever since he missed a heartbreakingly easy volley on match point in the National Junior Tennis Championships at the tender age of fifteen, he has been fascinated with the problem of how humans interfere with their own ability to achieve and learn.

Familiarity with these books and studies is an invaluable starting point to understanding the specific needs that plug into enhanced performance in a variety of sports. As noted above, I give clients some of the same suggestions offered conversationally by sports psychologists, but I deliver them when the clients are in a hypnotic state. I believe this approach has a more powerful effect (see the example in chapter 2 of a golfer who had previously worked with Dr. Rotella).

Sports psychologists typically focus on cognitive behavioral approaches to teach athletes the use of positive thoughts, or what might be referred to as effective thinking, during competition. My belief, however, is that hypnosis is an excellent example of how behavior can be changed first, through hypnotic intervention, which results in a shift in thinking—that is, working from a bottom-up (behavior-to-thinking) versus a top-down (thinking-to-behavior) approach. For example, if a client describes a fear of public speaking, a strictly cognitive therapist would probably attempt to alter the client's behaviors by changing his or her thinking about public speaking. My experience, however, is that by using hypnotic techniques to help clients feel relaxed and calm while giving a talk, their subsequent thinking about their effectiveness as a public speaker becomes much more positive. As a result, the fear or anxiety about public speaking dissipates naturally.

According to Williams and Leffingwell (2002), performance in sports as well as in other areas is affected by what athletes think about themselves, their situations, and their performances and how those thoughts then impact their feelings and behavior. I had some training in a sports hypnosis workshop with Dr. Lee Pulos and Mitch Smith (1998): I later did 3 workshops on Sports Hypnosis co-presented with Mitch Smith. According to Dr. Poulos, high-performance individuals know the power of self-talk. He says they have a system for programming themselves with positive messages that feed their cycle of self-esteem and self-confidence. Positive self-talk emphasizes what can be done versus what might go wrong. Negative self-chatter drains energy and creates toxic effects within individuals, while positive self-talk can create a psychic fountain that nourishes all aspects of one's being. According to Poulos, self-talk is nothing more than "everyday waking hypnosis."

Some sporting competitions happen so fast there isn't much time to think during the event (e.g., a hundred-meter sprint); others, however, allow space for a great deal of self-talk (e.g., endurance sports, such as distance running and triathlons). Golf, however, with the time between shots, is probably the most extreme example of a sport allowing for plenty of time for thinking positively or negatively.

An integral aspect of my approach is utilizing stories and anecdotes about great athletes. The goal is to focus on the importance of the mental aspect of their games. In his article titled "Mental Edge," Hodenfield (2009) refers to the fact that winning takes more than muscles, strategy, and execution; rather, "the ability to win often comes down to sheer, ice-cold nerve." He refers to a number of world-class athletes at the top of their games, such as tennis star Serena Williams, golf's Tiger Woods, skateboarding idol Tony Hawk, skier Lindsey Vonn, NASCAR driver Brian Vickers, and past football great John Elway. He includes the following quote from Serena Williams: "You have to have the desire to achieve, to do better and do more and continually do, do, do. It's an insatiable desire to not only win, but not to lose." While Tiger Woods has of late not performed quite as well as he once did, Hodenfield points out that few of Tiger's physical motions resemble those of his childhood hero, Jack Nicklaus. He notes, however, that the one tool they share is their most lethal weapon: "an unshakeable, unwavering ability to concentrate." He also refers to John Elway, the great quarterback for the Denver Broncos, who had an early induction into the Pro Football Hall of Fame only six years after his playing days ended in 1998. Elway is also a successful businessman. According to Hodenfield, Elway's business adviser reportedly said, "That ability to think quickly and process is what he used in his playing days when he read defenses quickly." He notes that this ability is probably why he was not only one of the greatest ever at the two-minute drill but also successful in business.

Billie Jean King is said to be one of the most famous female tennis players in history. In addition to having been a great female champion, she is widely known for her cross-gender match with Bobby Riggs. Many say that match opened the door for equal treatment of women in sports. In her book *Pressure Is a Privilege* (2008), King describes seeing pressure as a positive thing, which she refers to as "an opportunistic emotion." She says, "This produces energy and makes it easier to focus and concentrate on what is happening right now."

There are multiple reasons why I believe sports hypnosis is an attractive subspecialty of sports psychology. First, athletes are typically highly open to the need to change in a positive manner. In addition, the progress, gains, and successes are often dramatic and measurable. Perhaps more importantly, because athletes are so highly motivated to improve and are used to repetition in practicing their sports, they are usually equally receptive to the need to practice self-hypnosis as instructed.

Hypnotherapy's value in working with athletes who have had an injury and present with fear of or anxiety about competing is also evident. For example, the athlete can be desensitized in much the same manner as a phobic patient would be. Sometimes there are external factors limiting the athlete's success in competition. For example, a professional golfer with whom I worked had a specific psychological and financial reason behind why he kept barely failing to make the cut (this case is discussed in chapter 2).

Golf is highly popular internationally and across many age and ability levels, which likely accounts for why I have more requests for hypnosis from golfers than from athletes in any other sport. There appear to be many more participants, both amateur and professional, all of whom are seeking any method available to improve their golf scores.

The case examples are only a select few of the athletes to whom I have taught self-hypnosis techniques to realize their desire to improve their performance. Sports covered include golf; track and field (runners and jumpers); gymnastics and cheerleading; equestrian competition; baseball, basketball, and football (the US "big three"); softball; tennis; volleyball; soccer; and Olympic shooting. Techniques presented here can be adapted to work with any sport and, in fact, any competition or area in which performance enhancement is desired.

I discuss recovering from injury and returning to competition in chapter 8. If you are recovering from a lingering injury, working with someone with experience in the field of pain management is helpful. In the conclusion, I offer further suggestions regarding the generalization of these techniques and strategies for other areas in which peak performance is the goal.

For athletes who play or have played more than one sport, there is much crossover of information. An excellent example emerged in my interview with Brian Kinchen about his experiences in the 2003 Super Bowl. I had no idea beforehand what an avid and competitive golfer he was or how much of the interview he would spend talking about golf.

In chapter 2, I describe a telephone consult I had with a young golfer between his first and second days of competing in a world championship tournament. More recently, I had two telephone consults with an equestrian show jumper referred by equestrian coach Leaf Boswell. As a result of these experiences, which proved fruitful, I have been encouraged to work with other athletes traveling to compete in other states or countries. If you work with a hypnotherapist or plan to do so, I recommend asking him or her if phone consultations are an option.

In the scripts, you will note series of ellipses (i.e., "…"), which represent what I believe to be strategic pauses in the delivery of the script for emphasis or to allow you time to process what is being said. If you decide to make your own tape of the suggestions, you can also pause at these points for emphasis and for processing the suggestions.

A special note regarding the case examples: If I mention an athlete's name in a case example, I have received written consent from him or her to do so. Typically, these are athletes I have worked with in the past, and they are no longer clients and no longer competing. This fact is important so as not to create a dual relationship in which an endorsement is given by a current client, who then would serve as a marketing agent as well as a client.

Finally, I believe it is important to note that hypnosis does not provide extra talent to athletes; rather, it amplifies the talent they already have, giving greater access to as much of their talent as possible.

CHAPTER 1

Overview of Hypnotic and Self-Hypnotic Approaches in Sports

> Whether you think yourself a success, or you think yourself a failure, in either case, you're correct!
>
> —Anonymous

This quote is one of my favorites, not only for athletes but for all clients. Although the source is unknown, it sounds much like the work of Napoleon Hill in his book *Think and Grow Rich* (1938). Much of Hill's work is about meditation and focusing on what you would like to see happen in the future, whether in business, finance, or life. Some hypnotherapists refer to this as age progression. I often call it future projection, rehearsing future success, or future-focused therapy.

I use the same strategies and techniques to enter hypnosis with athletes as I do with other hypnotic applications (e.g., smoking cessation, alcohol and drug abuse treatment, weight loss, gambling, pain, and anxiety).

One of the first issues I address with an athlete who comes to my office—whether an adult who is a self-referral or a young athlete whose parents have encouraged him or her to see me—is to differentiate between psychotherapy and sports psychology. I explain that while I am trained as a clinical psychologist, seeing me does not imply that anyone thinks the client has a mental or emotional problem. Clinical psychologists often see people with mental or emotional problems, addictions, or other behavioral problems (kids typically know someone with attention deficit hyperactivity disorder [ADHD] who has seen a psychologist). But sports psychology is a subspecialty of psychology that does not involve these problems. I tell clients, "I'm not going to be your shrink, as some people call professionals like me. Rather, I would like you to think of me as your mental coach."

Since you have purchased this book, or someone purchased it for you, you are obviously aware of the above. One exception in my work was a professional golfer (see chapter 2) who was referred to me by a colleague who had diagnosed him with generalized anxiety disorder and obsessive-compulsive disorder. My colleague felt that hypnotherapy could help him with his clinical issues, but the client also wanted me to work with him on hypnotically enhanced achievement of peak performance. We decided we would focus first on the clinical issues and then later on his golf game.

While I spend time explaining hypnosis to all my clients, my belief is that a good orientation to hypnosis and self-hypnosis is especially important with the athlete client. My reasoning is that athletes spend so much time being coached on the mechanics of their respective sports that I want them to get a feel for the mental mechanics of hypnosis. To begin, I think of hypnosis as involving two components. First, hypnosis is the art of getting the client (or oneself in self-hypnosis) into a hypnotic state. Second, the therapy component involves what is done once the client (or self) is in hypnosis. The following section of the book represents the lens through which I see hypnosis working as I understand it and how I like to explain it.

When clients come to my office, we first discuss their presenting concerns and determine the goals they wish to achieve. In this phase of information gathering, I always ask two basic questions:

1. What percentage of success in golf is mental?
2. What percentage of your time do you spend on the mental aspects of your performance and competition?

Often, the answer to question one is very high—50, 75, or even 90 percent—and the answer to question two is zero. The lesson here is that I am going to be a mental coach.

Then I tell athletes the same story I relate to all my new clients, even when hypnosis or performance enhancement is not a consideration. The anecdote is perhaps even more significant for athletes because I use a coaching metaphor.

A number of years ago, a young man came in for his first psychotherapy session with me. I noticed from his information sheet that he had not been in therapy before. He was kind of fidgety and was shuffling his feet. I asked him if he felt a little uncomfortable in being there. He said, "Yeah, man. I don't know if I'm wasting your time and mine."

I responded, "I know. Guys are supposed to solve their own problems, right?" He agreed, and I continued. "And big boys don't cry, right?" Again, he nodded in agreement.

Well, lucky for me, at that time of year, the Summer Olympics were going on. Coincidentally, the Summer Olympics are on the same four-year rotation as US presidential campaigns for the November elections, so the races were heating up. I asked, "Did you read the newspaper today?" After he acknowledged that he had, I asked, "Did you read about the Olympic athletes?"

He responded, "Oh yes. I love the Summer Olympics. I can't wait to get home from work every evening to watch them on TV."

I asked, "Did you read about all of the presidential candidates?"

He said he had.

I said, "I'll bet everyone you read about who was good at anything had someone working with him or her behind the scenes to get better. The athletes all have coaches. The candidates have advisers, campaign managers, and speechwriters. Actors and actresses have directors. Anybody who is good at anything has someone helping him or her get better.

"Mike Tyson was heavyweight champion of the world before he went crazy and started biting people's ears off. But even Mike had a little old man in his corner reminding him to keep up his left, move, and so on. Mike already knew he had to keep up his left, but sometimes it helps to have someone objective looking in and giving guidance. And that is how I see therapy. It is like having a coach but one who coaches or consults with you regarding life's issues or problems you want to change."

The metaphor worked so well with the client that I began using it with many of my new clients, regardless of the presenting problem and regardless of gender. With a female competitor, for example, I might say, "Competitors like yourself are supposed to solve their own problems, right?" The idea of a mental coach is accepted particularly well by adolescents, and it is not gender specific. With athletes, I often modify the ending of the story since we are not speaking metaphorically but, rather, directly regarding their seeing me as a mental coach.

If you wonder whether you can be hypnotized, my standard answer is "Anybody bright and creative can be hypnotized." Not surprisingly, most clients typically accept this perspective. I always follow with "Only once has a client called my bluff by saying, 'Oh well, I guess that leaves me out!' As it turned out, she was a very bright and witty woman just making a joke, and she was an excellent hypnotic subject."

Regardless of why a client wants to be hypnotized—whether to enhance performance, quit smoking, lose weight, deal with other addictions, control pain, learn a technique adjunctive to other psychotherapy, or achieve something else—I always start off by providing an overview, even if the client has been hypnotized by someone else in the past. This summary presents my particular philosophy about hypnosis and how it works. When describing to the client what hypnosis is, I often find myself talking about what it is not.

Many people only have the image of stage hypnotists who try to convince their spectators that they can use hypnosis to control the minds of individual members of the audience and make them do silly things, such as crawl around like a chicken and cluck, but in medical and psychological hypnosis, the idea is that I, the mental coach, cannot control your mind, nor would I want to, but I can teach you to use your own mind power to achieve your goals. The key is your mind power, not mine, and your goals, not mine. I serve only as a teacher or guide. I can't hypnotize you against your will, so in a way, all hypnosis is self-hypnosis. You have to be a willing participant. You have to want to do it.

Hypnosis is an altered state of consciousness. It is not an unconscious state. The name is a misnomer. It comes from the Greek word *hypnos*, which means "sleep." The Greek god Hypnos was the god of sleep. But you will not be asleep. You will be very much awake. Your eyes will be closed but only to block out distractions, just as a music lover might put on headphones and close his or her eyes to focus more intently on the audio and block out visual distractions. You will hear everything I say. You will be able to talk back if I ask you questions. You will remember everything we talk about, unless there is some reason to block it out. When your mind and body are totally relaxed, you can concentrate better on everything I say and on whatever we are dealing with—in this case, suggestions about sports performance.

If you were to see me in my office, I would say, "Before you leave today, I will give you two brochures about hypnosis. The first is *Questions and Answers about Clinical Hypnosis*, published by Ohio Publishing. It was prepared by William Wester, a longtime faculty member of the American Society of Clinical Hypnosis. The second is *Hypnosis: What It Is and How It Can Make You Feel Better*, published by Division 30 of the American Psychological Association, the Society of Psychological Hypnosis." You can probably find both brochures online should you desire more information.

I then would present the following techniques for orientation.

Hypnotic Suggestibility Test

This is not hypnosis but, rather, a test of visual imagery, since so much of our work will deal with visualization.

> Close your eyes. Settle back and relax. Now I want you to imagine sitting on a beach on a beautiful spring or summer day. Perhaps you're sitting on a beach towel or blanket or a recliner. Imagine enjoying the beautiful

weather. You feel the warm sunshine on your skin. There is a nice breeze coming off the water. You are enjoying the weather and the scenery.

I want you to imagine there are some children playing nearby, near the water's edge. They are little children—perhaps children you know, or they could be total strangers … They are playing with little sand buckets and shovels … When I was a kid, these buckets were usually made of some kind of metal material, tin or aluminum. Nowadays they are typically plastic or rubberized. But they all have one thing in common: a little curved handle so a child can carry the bucket.

I invite you to imagine that one of the children comes over to you and asks you to put out your arms. You go ahead and do so. Imagine the child then places the bucket over the top of one of your wrists so that it hangs from your wrist like a giant bracelet. Then the child starts filling the bucket with sand.

As the child does so, the bucket becomes heavier and heavier … The natural pull of gravity causes the bucket to feel heavier. As it gets heavier, the bucket gradually causes your arm to descend down toward the ground, toward the sand below … It is getting really heavy, and you would like to hold it up for the child, but you feel it getting heavier and heavier … It is about one-third full and getting really heavy … Now the child starts filling it with wet sand, and wet sand is even heavier than dry sand because it is denser … The bucket is about half full and now really heavy.

Now open your eyes, and look at your arms.

By this time, the arm has typically descended somewhat. Usually, one arm has descended noticeably. If the arm has not descended, it likely is sore from holding up the bucket.

This approach is followed by what I refer to as a muscle-testing demonstration. You can practice this on a friend if you would like.

> When I tell you to put out your arm, I want you to hold out one arm, the one closer to me. After I describe something to you, I want you to make it very rigid, and when I try to push your arm down, I want you to resist to the best of your ability.
>
> Now I want you to think about the greatest accomplishment in your whole life—something you are proud of and would be happy for everyone to know about. It could be an award, achievement, or accomplishment. You would be happy to see it published on the front page of the local newspaper or in a newsletter of some sort. Nod when you have something in mind. [Wait for the nod.] Now resist.

Invariably, the person will show great power to resist his or her arm being pushed down.

> Now relax the arm for a while. Now I want you to think about the lowest, most low-down, most rotten thing you have ever done in your life—something you did that you should not have done or something you should have done but didn't, something you are embarrassed about and wouldn't want anyone to know about. Everyone has something … Nod when you have that in mind. [Wait for the nod.] Now make your arm rigid again, keep that negative thought in mind, and resist when I try to push your arm down.

Invariably, one's arm is easily pushed down with this imagery.

I often tell a story about using this technique as a demonstration to the athletic department at the University of New Orleans. I had worked with a varsity volleyball player who, after just three sessions, had her best game ever. The local newspaper wrote that she'd achieved a career high in digs. I didn't even know what a dig was but soon found out it was a defensive save.

When the coaches learned that I had taught her self-hypnosis, they invited me to give a presentation to the athletic department. I used the technique, asking for a volunteer from the audience. The women's basketball coach volunteered. He was tall and very muscular. I whispered in his ear the first instruction regarding thinking about something he was proud of. I then practically hung from his arm and could not budge it. Then I whispered the negative suggestion, and that time, his arm went down immediately and easily.

The purpose of the exercise is to instill confidence in the hypnotic approach by showing that the person is likely to be a good hypnotic subject. I tell many athletes the following additional story.

For five years, I coached marathon teams for the Leukemia and Lymphoma Society's fundraising campaign called Team in Training (TNT). The runners would raise money for treatment and research, and in exchange for their raising X amount of money, the society would pay their airfare, hotel, and entry fees to a marathon, usually in a nice place to visit, such as Disney World, San Diego, San Francisco, Bermuda, or Maui. The society would pay for a pasta dinner the evening before the race, and last but not least, they would provide a running coach.

I was the coach for the Mississippi Gulf Coast Team for five years, and I took runners to approximately fifteen different marathons. The entrants had varying degrees of running experience, from veteran marathoners to first-timers. Some had run 5Ks, 10Ks, or even half-marathons, but some had never run competitively. We would train as a team every Saturday, but in between, they were to train on their own or in smaller groups, following a training schedule I had prepared for them.

Runner's World magazine was one of TNT's sponsors and donated training logs. The runners were instructed to keep a daily and weekly record of their running—for example, the number of miles, conditions, and any cross-training. They were to run five days per week and cross-train two days (e.g., lift weights, bike, or swim).

At the bottom of each weekly page was a quote. Of course, there are many quotes about running that have to do with life in general. Probably the most famous one is "Life is a marathon, not a sprint." You have heard that one before, haven't you? One week, the quote was as follows: "Whether you think yourself a success, or you think yourself a failure, in either case, you're correct!" When I read that, I thought about how much it applied to my general psychological practice but also, perhaps even more specifically, to athletes. The key message here is that change is possible.

To reiterate how the mental side of competition affects athletes in all sports, there was recently an Associated Press article about Simona Halep's collapse in 2018 at Wimbledon. She had been ranked and seeded number one, fresh off winning the French Open. After that win, she'd said she was sure she had figured out how to overcome "big-moment anxiety," as she called it, which had been so problematic for her for so long.

The article noted that she chastised herself for being "unprofessional" after bowing out in the third round. She lost the last five games to Hsieh Su-Wei of Taipan. She said, "I was just too negative to myself, talking too much. I think because I was tired, because I'm tired, I couldn't stay focused for every ball." She added, "Mentally I was tired. Also physically, I feel tired. My muscles are gone."

The writer of the article wrote, "Simona Halep was ready for a vacation. It's going to start a week earlier than she wanted after she gave away a big lead, wasted a match point and lost at Wimbledon, joining a procession of top women on the way out."

This account reminds me of watching LeBron James in the NBA finals a couple of years ago. He often played the entire game with little, if any, breaks on the bench. Is he just that much more physically in shape than the other players? I think not. What sets him apart is upstairs.

The Quiet Eye (QE)

In a June 29, 2018, BBC feature article titled "Why Athletes Need a 'Quiet Eye,'" the author noted, "If anyone knows how to grab victory from the jaws of defeat, it's Serena Williams." He referred to her semifinal match against Kim Clijsters at the 2003 Australian Open. She was down 5–2 in the final set, but rather than slipping into despair and losing her place in the tournament, she saved two match points before winning the next five games. He noted that Serena made similar breathtaking comebacks at the 2005 Australian Open, 2009 Wimbledon, and 2014 China Open. He said in each case, the extreme pressure only seemed to sharpen her concentration.

The author, David Robson, said psychologists and neuroscientists have now identified some common mental processes that mark out elite athletes, one of which is known as the quiet eye, a kind of enhanced visual perception that allows athletes to eliminate distractions as they plan their next move. It apparently is even more important at times of stress, preventing choking under pressure.

The writer explains that there is a small window of opportunity for the motor system to receive information from the eyes, and experts have found a way to optimize that window. He notes that Joan Vickers, herself an athlete, hooked a group of professional golfers to a device that precisely monitored their eye movements as they putted. What she found was intriguing: the better the golfer was (as measured by golf handicap), the longer and steadier his or her gaze on the ball just before and then during his or her strike. Less sophisticated and experienced golfers, on the other hand, tended to shift their focus between different areas of the scene, with each fixation lasting for shorter periods of time.

The general idea of keeping your eye on the ball is preached by coaches in all sports, but this idea of the quiet eye suggests something much more intense.

Experiments have shown that quiet-eye training has improved athletes in basketball, volleyball, and Olympic skeet shooting. In 2017, the *European Journal of Sport Science* devoted a whole issue to exploring this phenomenon. One writer on the subject theorized that it involves advanced intelligence gathering—that is, the quiet eye allows one to "soak in all the information from the object in question," which "helps you to produce the best motor response (Sáenz-Moncaleano et al. 2016). The article suggests this period of focus is especially crucial in high-stakes situations, preventing the athlete from choking.

Some have suggested the QE duration correlates with self-reported feelings of flow or being in the zone, or in other words, the sensation of effortless concentration in which your mind is clear of everything except the task at hand. The idea is that the QE filters distractions and calms the mind and the body at the critical moment, even under stress. In this state, it is apparent that heart rate temporarily decelerates, and the movement of the limbs becomes smoother.

Consistent with the above statement about flow, a recent research study published in the *International Journal of Clinical and Experimental Hypnosis* looked at the relationship between flow and hypnotizability (Bowers, Na, and Elkins 2018). Flow, in this case, is considered a specific brain state in order to focus one's attention on the task at hand, maximizing skill and efficiency. Some have described this state as commonly associated with hypnosis, meditation, and the so-called runner's high. The study suggested that hypnosis may be used to induce a state of flow and thereby improve performance. In summary, the results suggested people who have a higher hypnotic ability are more prone to report flow-like experiences in hypnosis. In my mind, this all equates to being in the zone, so to speak.

Serena Williams once said, "I've won most of my matches—probably all of my grand slams—because of what's upstairs, not anything else." She said that when she is behind in a game, that's when she becomes most relaxed. Her statement of "what's upstairs" is akin to what I mentioned above about LeBron James in basketball.

Again, let me summarize for those of you who purchased this book to improve your golf game and wonder, *Why this talk about tennis and other sports?* Because the mental side of any sport is all-important. It is the difference between good players and champions. Many have the physical tools, but those with the mental toughness are the ones who become champions.

Synchronicity, or There Are No Coincidences

Several years ago, I presented a workshop on sports hypnosis at a national hypnosis society meeting. On the shuttle to the airport after the conference ended, husband and wife psychologists were sitting next to me and asked what I had spoken about (obviously, they had not attended my workshop, as there had been several going on simultaneously). When I told them, the wife said she was sorry she'd missed it, because it sounded interesting. Then she asked if I had ever read *Golf in the Kingdom* (1972; 1997) by Michael Murphy. I said I had not but would check it out.

I purchased a used copy of the book, and it sat on my dresser for about three years, as there were many other books I read during that time about a variety of topics. Finally, while writing this manuscript, I decided maybe I should see what all the fuss was about and picked up Murphy's book. I'm glad I made that decision.

As the story goes, the author was on his way to study philosophy in India but planned a stop in Scotland to play at a legendary golf club, and the experience transformed his life. The book, according to *Wikipedia*, has sold more than a million copies and has been translated into nineteen languages.

Michael Murphy is a graduate of Stanford University and cofounder and chairman emeritus of the board of the Esalen Institute, and he directs the institute's think-tank operations through its Center for Theory and Research (CTR). The Esalen Institute in California, commonly called Esalen, played a key role in the human potential movement beginning in the 1960s. This movement led to what was later called humanistic psychology. Murphy is also the author of four novels, including *Golf in the Kingdom.*

Amazon's description of *Golf in the Kingdom* says it has been recognized as a classic work on the deeper mysteries of golf—a gospel of those who suspect, or know, that golf is more than a mere pastime. In the book, a young man in route to India stops in Scotland to play at the legendary Burningbush golf club, and in twenty-four hours, his life is transformed. Paired with a mysterious teacher named Shivas Irons, he is led through a round of phenomenal golf, swept into a world where extraordinary powers are unleashed in a backswing governed by what the teacher refers to as "true gravity." A night of adventure and revelation follows and leads to a glimpse of Seamus MacDuff, the holy man who haunts a ravine off Burningbush's thirteenth fairway, which locals call Lucifer's Rug. Murphy's account reveals the possibilities for transcendence that reside in the human soul, and through mystic philosopher Shivas Irons, the reader, like Murphy, is drawn into new worlds by the ancient and haunting game.

Burningbush, of course, is not the real name. Murphy describes the golfing links as being in the Kingdom of Fife, on the shore of the North Sea. Others commenting on the book have thought it perhaps is Balcomie Links or perhaps even the legendary Saint Andrews.

There, Murphy met the aforementioned golf professional and teacher named Shivas Irons, and he describes many lessons he learned from the philosopher golfer that impacted not only his golf game but also the rest of his life. One such lesson was to "wait 'em oot [out]," a lesson in patience.

Shivas talked about men being hypnotized by the game, which made Murphy think, *Why not use hypnosis?* Shivas said we must remember that "hypnosis is first cousin to fascination."

The above-mentioned Seamus MacDuff was supposedly a mentor to Shivas. Shivas reportedly said Seamus taught him "life is nothin' but a series of fascinations, an odyssey from world to world. And so with golf. An odyssey as it is—from hole to hole, adventure after adventure, comic and tragic, spellin' out the human drama."

He added,

> Gowf [golf] is a place to practice fascination—it is slow enough to concentrate the mind and complex enough to

> require our many parts—tis a microcross of the world's larger discipline. Our feelin's, fantasies, thoughts and muscles, all must join to play. In 'gowf' ye see the essence of what the world itself demands. Inclusion of all our parts, alignment o' them all with one another and with the club and with the ball, with all the land we play on and with our playin' partners.

Murphy goes on to include weather, subtle energies that change each day, and the feelings of those around us. He notes that we are rewarded when we bring them all together and treated badly when we don't.

Why do I refer in the above section title to synchronicity? First, the woman who recommended the book to me does not, as far as I know, work in the field of sports psychology, or she likely would have attended my presentation. Second, I had no idea the book had such an emphasis on metaphysical or psychic phenomena. Further, because I had some prior training in metaphysical and psychic phenomena, the wisdom of the mystic masters, and so on, Michael Murphy's book was much more appealing to me than it might have been to someone without that background. For readers who are strict pragmatists focused on "Prove it, and I'll believe it" science, as most psychologists are, Murphy's book might not appear to have much value. On the other hand, if you have come to believe, as have I, that science often doesn't even know what questions to ask, much less how to find the answers, the book opens another whole world of possibilities.

In summary, all of the above is intended to demonstrate to you how important the mental side of sport is, as well as how self-hypnosis training can bring you to your highest mental state. This fact holds true whether you are a professional golfer or an amateur just playing for fun. I wonder how many in the latter group truly do not have a strong competitive spirit.

CHAPTER 2

Self-Hypnosis for Golfers

> Life isn't about waiting for the storm to pass …
> It's about learning to dance in the rain.
>
> —Vivian Greene

> Shallow men believe in luck. Strong men believe in cause and effect.
>
> —Ralph Waldo Emerson

Is a Formal Hypnotic Trance Necessary to Have a Hypnotic Effect?

On a Saturday evening in a restaurant and bar in Bay St. Louis, Mississippi, a friend and I were having an after-dinner drink at the bar. Being a friendly person, my friend started a conversation with the couple sitting to her left. The man said they had moved to the Mississippi Gulf Coast area from Tampa, where his son was now running his business, a golf pro shop. When she told him I was in the process of writing a book about hypnosis for golfers, he showed some interest. We never did find out his name. I surmised he had at one time been a professional golfer and perhaps had at some point been on tour. I proceeded to tell him a story I often tell people to show that a hypnotic effect does not have to be elicited through a formal hypnotic trance.

A good friend of mine is a pretty good amateur golfer. For quite some time, he had been saying he wanted me to hypnotize him to help him relax on the course. I had heard that his friends didn't want to play with him anymore because of his temper while playing, and he told me he'd found himself grasping the club so hard the veins popped out on his arms.

But he always made his request at inopportune times, like if we were out at dinner with other people. One weekend, he and his friends were playing in a tournament on the Mississippi Gulf Coast. Rather than staying at the hotel with the other golfers, he stayed at my house, as we had planned. On Friday evening, we went to a casino, had drinks, and had a good time. Saturday morning, while we were having coffee, he asked, "Can you hypnotize me to make me play better today?"

I knew he only had about fifteen minutes before he had to leave for the course in order to make his tee time, so I said, "No, I can't do anything that quickly. We should have worked on this last night!"

He said, "Aw man, I forgot all about it."

After I thought about it for a minute, however, I said, "Wait. There is something you can do. When you are about to take your shot, take a deep breath, which will allow more oxygen to get to your brain; smile, because the facial movements involved in smiling also allow more oxygen to the brain—that is why humor is so therapeutic; and tell yourself everything is going to be fine. And if nothing else, the guys you're playing with, who know you quite well, are going to wonder what you are smiling about."

He called later that day and said, "You're not going to believe this. I won the whole thing."

I asked about the other players' reactions, and he said, "They kept asking, 'What the hell are you so happy about?'"

The guy at the bar said he had been watching the LPGA earlier that day, and a girl from Thailand atop the leaderboard had given a big smile before every shot. I later checked it out on Sunday evening and saw her name was Ariya Jutanugarn. The event was the 2018 Ladies Scottish Open, which she won. As I was leaving the bar, the guy said, "Nice talking to you, and thanks for the tip. I'm going to smile more!"

In my first draft of the chapter on golf for my previous book, I made the following statement:

> Let me begin by noting that I have never worked with a champion or so-called elite golfer. I have, however, worked with golfers at many levels, including professionals, one of whom made the LPGA qualifying tournament and another of whom played for a couple of years on an Asian tour, and all of them reported improved performance following the experience. This fact is likely to be especially pertinent to those golfers who are not professional, much less champions, but good enough to aspire to go professional or even to get better and to achieve peak performance while continuing to play at the amateur level.

After that draft, however, I had the privilege of working with a young girl who won a world championship in her age group. The experience was delightful because of her motivation, dedication, and insightfulness, as well as her ability to generalize the techniques I taught her from the golf course to the classroom.

Furthermore, I recently worked with a professional golfer (described in case number four) and, more recently, one who was in the qualifying round for the PGA.

Before getting into the specific techniques used with golfers, I will present five case examples. A college golfer with whom I worked until recently reported he is doing well with the techniques. I cannot give identifying information about him or any current client, because as I noted earlier, doing so would put them in a mixed role of being my client and marketing for me, which is forbidden by the American Psychological Association's ethics code regarding dual relationships.

The five cases follow.

Case One: My First Athlete Client

A professional golfer was the first athlete I ever used hypnosis with back in 1984. He was referred to me by a mutual acquaintance who was one of his supporters and who paid for his sessions with me. His case was some twenty-five years before my 2011 book, and all of the files in my Mississippi Gulf Coast office were lost in Hurricane Katrina, but I remember him well. Since I had not worked with a golfer before and, in fact, had just learned to use hypnosis for performance enhancement, his sponsor gave me a copy of Timothy Gallwey's 1981 book *The Inner Game of Golf.*

I quickly read the book before the first session. The client said that in every tournament qualifying round, he would do fine until the last hole or two, and then he would blow up and miss the qualifying cut by one stroke. His situation sounded a lot like Gallwey's discussion of athletes creating their own obstacles to achievement.

In our first session, my focus was primarily on introducing him to hypnosis and relaxation training, in addition to deep-breathing techniques, with suggestions regarding generalizing the techniques to his golf game. By the second session, I felt it important to use hypnotic regression to uncover what was causing him to trip himself up just before qualifying. I regressed him to his most recent tournament and helped him review what thoughts were going through his head just before the final hole. The results were interesting. He said his sponsorship money had basically run out; he had no savings; and he knew that if he qualified, he did not have enough money to even stay in a hotel and buy meals throughout the rest of the tournament.

What followed was not hypnosis, nor was it psychotherapy. I called my amateur golfer friend in New Orleans, who was a businessman, was always passionate about golf, and later served as a committee member for the Zurich Classic in New Orleans. Once made aware of the situation, he arranged for my client to come to New Orleans and play with some of his businessmen golfing friends, who wound up sponsoring him for a while. After another hypnotic session or two, during which I attempted to hypnotically reinforce some of the concepts I'd learned from Gallwey's book, he experienced success.

While working with him, I explained that my focus with him was not on the mechanics of his game, which he already knew and which his golf coach could help him tweak, but on the mental aspects. In his next competition, which was a small local tournament in Hattiesburg, Mississippi, he not only qualified but won first-place money. Later, after he gave me a few free golf lessons, I heard he was on the Asian Tour.

Because that experience was so long ago and I no longer have paper records but wanted to include my first case of using sports hypnosis in this chapter, I tracked him down for a telephone interview. I explained that I wanted to include my work with him in a book and wanted to know if he felt the hypnotic experience had helped. If it had, I wanted him to tell me in his own words how it had helped. After saying, "Good to hear from you, Dr. Joe," he told me, "My biggest mistake was not staying with you a little longer. The best I ever played was after we worked together a couple of times. The first few tournaments after that was the best I ever played! I had a 74.1 average in '83 and '84 and lowered it to 71.6 in '86 and '87."

He reported that in the Hattiesburg tournament he won after seeing me, he would play a round and then wake up after the last hole. He added, "I was focused on hitting the ball and then totally forgetting golf. You told me that whether the shot was good or bad, I should focus on something else: the water if near an ocean, the trees, or birds. Anything but golf! In one round, I remember finishing several strokes ahead of the field and not remembering the round because I was so focused."

I'd learned that advice from reading Gallwey's book. Gallwey notes that a tennis player is hitting a moving ball over and over again on the run, and a skier is hurtling down a mountain slope, so their reactions are much more instinctual than mental. The difference in golf, however, is that the golfer has much more time to think between shots. If the previous shot was a bad one, negative thoughts might involve grappling with self-doubt, anxiety, fear of failure, tension, and other negative self-talk. I saw a similar difference between working with sprinters and working with distance runners, as described in chapter 4 of my previous book on sports hypnosis. In most sports, as will be seen later, too much time spent thinking about a previous shot, good or bad, might distract the player.

My former client noted, "Back then, unless they were on the PGA Tour, few people could make enough money to survive, even on the Asian Tour." He met a girl from Jackson, Mississippi, in about 1987; quit playing; got married; and started working as a golf pro and then as a real estate agent. At the time of our interview, he was a stock trader. He said, "It was tough quitting. I wish I had stuck with you longer." He asked me if I had watched the 2009 Masters, which had been on the weekend before our interview. He said, "Several of the leaders melted in the last two holes; they could have used your help!"

In the April 20, 2009, issue of *Sports Illustrated*, the feature article was titled "Last Man Standing" (Shipnuck 2009, 30–34). The writer discussed the events and twists at the end of that Masters that led to Angel Cabrera's victory. The cover of that edition was interesting. The headline read, "The Masters: Angel and the Bedeviled."

Star Power, or What Do the Elite Golfers Do Differently?

In the article "Mental Edge," referenced in chapter 1, Hodenfield reports, "In the nerve-wracking game of pro golf, Nicklaus' method—which he talked about openly—was to do the very best he could against the course and just let the other guys fall apart like a cardboard suitcase. When the pressure was loaded on, they usually did." Hodenfield says, "Tom Weiskopf, Nicklaus' long-suffering rival, said: 'Jack knew he was going to beat you. You knew Jack was going to beat you. And Jack knew that you knew he was going to beat you.'" He adds, "And Tiger is hearing the same music now."

That article was written in 2009. Unfortunately, a number of things on and off the course seemingly have caused Tiger Woods, who at one time was considered the greatest living athlete, to perform at a lesser level than before. I read with much interest a recent article in *USA Today* in which the author, Steve DiMeglio, talks about the 2008 US Open

(2018). The article was printed shortly before the 2018 British Open, and the title is "'08 US Open a Great Tiger Tale." DiMeglio says that in that tournament, "Tiger Woods delivered the most astonishing performance in a career filled with spectacular acts of genius, power, artistry and relentless determination." He talks about how Tiger beat back a field of the world's best players and somehow overcame excruciating pain to win his fourteenth major championship. He had stress fractures in his left tibia and torn ligaments in his left knee. He was said to grimace, limp, and, at times, stagger through five days of golf to join Jack Nicklaus as one of only two players to win the career Grand Slam three times over. Dottie Pepper, a two-time majors champion who won the Best Female Golfer ESPY Award in 1993 and is now a television golf broadcaster, dubbed it "one of the greatest achievements in the history of sports." Up to the date of that article, he'd won his last major title in 2008.

After reading the above article, I paid special attention to the 2018 British Open, in which Tiger finished in a tie for sixth with a total score of five under, three strokes behind the winner, Francesco Molinari. A writer from PGA.com wrote that Tiger was in contention until the very end and was said to look like the "Tiger of old" on several occasions. After the seventh hole on the last round, he was just one shot off the lead, and the writer said, "Is this really happening?"

After nine holes, the writer said, "Spieth is crumbling, and Tiger is atop the leaderboard. This is not a drill, folks."

Tiger then faded on the back nine with a double bogey on eleven and a bogey on twelve. Many sportswriters seemed to believe he had turned a corner and would win another major.

Subsequently, Tiger closed with a 64 at the PGA Championship at Bellerive. He finished at 266, breaking by three shots his personal best over 72 holes in a major. While neither score was enough to win the tournament, Tiger finished second overall. He last had won a major ten years before, and his last victory of any variety had been five years before. Tiger was quoted as once saying it could not be considered a truly great year without winning a major. Now, however, we had to believe it was a good year as he continued to progress. In my competitive running years (during which I ran 5Ks, 10Ks, half-marathons, and three full marathons), we runners always were striving to set a new personal record (PR), or personal best. We basically were competing with ourselves.

I think Tiger must be pleased that although he got second, he set a PR. As I write this book, I keep adding more about his progression, and I suspect that by the time the book makes it to print, he will have won another major.

In summary, Tiger's resurrection demonstrates to all golfers the importance of the mental side of the game.

Case Two: Female Golfer Who Had Been All SEC in 2000 and in the LPGA Qualifying Round

Lisette Lee (now Prieto), a female golfer who was in the qualifying school for the LPGA, worked with me on two occasions in my New Orleans office in 2002. Lisette had been an excellent college golfer selected to the All-SEC team in 2000 and named SEC athlete of the week twice that year. She'd had ten top-ten finishes. In addition, in 2000, she'd received the Dinah Shores Trophy sponsored by the LPGA Foundation. As a senior at LSU, she also had received the Boyd McWhorter SEC Scholar-Athlete Award.

Once again, because I lost my paper files in Hurricane Katrina, I wanted to interview Lisette to ask her about her recollections of our work together; if it had helped; and, if so, what memories she had about how it had helped. My good friend in New Orleans, who was the one who originally referred her to me, was able to help me get in touch with her. He had been a member of the Zurich Classic committee and a chairperson of that committee in 2010. At the time, I learned that she had been on the committee with him.

When I talked with her, she reminded me that in addition to the information I listed above, during the summer of 1996, between her senior year in high school and her freshman year at LSU, she played in the US Open. She later married a man who was a caddie for a female golfer who has since made it to the LPGA tour, and her husband was a teaching pro at a country club. At the time of our interview, they had a son who was twenty months old and another on the way. She reported that she had not been competing or even playing much. She did remember vividly, however, her two sessions with me nearly seven years prior to our interview.

In addition, she gave me more background about her experience. She was on the LPGA Futures Tour from 2000 to 2003, and her best finish, twelfth place, was in 2001. She noted, "I was too focused on the money and put extra stress on myself." She added, "In 2002, after working with you, I made it to the final stage at qualifying but missed the cut by one shot." The night before the final round, after thinking she'd made it, she was notified there had been a bad ruling. "I had to add another stroke, so I missed the cut by one," she said.

The below question-and-answer interview session followed.

JT: Do you think the hypnosis training helped?

LL: Absolutely! I remember you counting me down from ten to one, and an elevator, and a staircase. I remember using the techniques to bring my emotions, which there were a lot of, into a controlled state. It obviously worked, because I'd tried to qualify in 2000 and in 2001 and never made it past the first stage. It helped me calm down and focus. And I made it to the finals. I remember the deep-breathing exercises really helped me a lot, especially on the first hole. That first hole is probably the most nervous you'll ever be. For me, it wasn't the tee shot. It was the walk from the tee to the second shot of the first hole. That is when the deep breathing—you told me all the way from my stomach—calmed down my emotions.

JT: Do you remember us talking about visualizing the next shot and then, when it was over, letting it go so that thinking about the last shot, whether it was good or bad, would not interfere with the next one?

LL: Yes, I remember those two techniques. I had forgotten, but now that you mention them, I remember using them. Visualization really helped. I would picture the shot before I hit it or even before my practice swing and would even visualize the flight of the ball. The mental part of golf is so important. That's why Tiger Woods is so much better than the others. Of course, he is a good striker, but they all are. He is just so mentally good!

JT: Anything else?

LL: I just ran out of money and couldn't continue.

During the interview, I got the distinct impression our dialogue reminded Lisette of how much she missed the competition, and I mused, *Who knows? She is still young.*

Case Three: The College Player

Another promising player with whom I worked was a young man who had just received a golf scholarship to a prestigious Catholic university in the Midwest. Notably, during our interview, the young man said that after just a few sessions with me, he scored his lowest score ever. In his case, and in other cases with golfers, I used many of the suggestions that famous sports psychologist Dr. Bob Rotella gives to his golfer clients, although I gave them to him while he was in a hypnotic state. He proved to be a good hypnotic subject. Interestingly, the young golfer informed me that Dr. Rotella was a family friend, and he'd had some sessions with Dr. Bob, as he called him, in which he was given many of the same suggestions conversationally. He said, however, he never played as well as he did after being given the suggestions hypnotically. I said, "Well, when you talk to Dr. Bob again, tell him about this experience."

My intention here is not in any way to discredit Dr. Rotella, as he is a highly respected sports psychologist, and I have learned much from his books. Rather, my intent is to reinforce the power of hypnotic suggestion.

Case Four: Emotional Distress and Peak-Performance Issues

This case is noteworthy because of the presence of emotional distress along with the professional golfer's problems in competition. It became apparent that his level of emotional distress was the first thing that needed treatment. It was also obvious he would have trouble focusing on his golf game while he was suffering from clinically significant generalized anxiety disorder as well as a number of interpersonal and relationship problems. Initially, we had to deal with his clinical anxiety. I discussed with him Selye's (1956) description of panic attacks, the so-called fight-or-flight response. Then hypnotherapy was implemented. In such cases, I often use a metaphor I call "the master control room metaphor" to help patients get over anxiety. This technique is similar to one I use for lowering subjective pain (see chapter 8). The client is told the following:

> I invite you to imagine you can go to a place in your own brain ... At Epcot Center, there was a ride, which no longer exists, in which you were in a chamber that was a replica of the inside of a spaceship. The patrons were harnessed in, as you might be in a spaceship, and then there was a simulation of a spaceship taking off. The ride included sounds and the feeling of centrifugal force pinning you back against the seat—a good simulation of a spaceship taking off. Then, after liftoff, the ship shot through a barrier and shrank to a miniature state, and you were projected inside the human body,

where you studied the heart, lungs, and more. It was an educational ride.

Let's suppose a miniature you could be projected inside your own brain. I think of the brain as the control center of the body. I imagine it as being much like a NASA space center. I've never been to a NASA facility, but I have seen movies about astronauts, and the astronauts are always communicating with the space center in Houston, as in "Come in, Houston." Imagine you can go inside this control center … in your brain. The brain is, in fact, your control center … Imagine you come upon a lot of technical instruments: monitors, gauges, controls, and switches.

You see a monitor on the left … that has a gauge for tension, stress, or anxiety … They all mean pretty much the same thing … Just to the right, there is a monitor for calm and relaxation … Imagine that at first, the level on the left gauge, tension or anxiety, is a nine on a ten-point scale … The one on the right, the relaxation scale, is a one … Imagine you then begin to adjust the levels … There are knobs like rheostats … As you turn the relaxation knob clockwise from a one to a two with your right hand, you turn the anxiety and tension knob counterclockwise to an eight with your left hand. Next, you turn the relaxation gauge up to a three and simultaneously turn the tension gauge down to a seven … You notice the difference.

You continue turning the relaxation gauge up to a four, but as you are about to turn the tension down to a six, you notice an interesting phenomenon: that knob seems to be turning by itself automatically … This is understandable because tension and relaxation are incompatible responses. They are what we call mutually exclusive … You can't be tense when you're relaxed … And you can't be relaxed when you're tense.

You interestedly proceed … You turn the relaxation control up to a five, and the tension automatically reduces to a five … Excited, you continue the process … You turn the relaxation up to a six, and the tension goes down to a four … Then they are a seven and a three and so on. You might take them all the way to a nine and a one, as a perfect ten and zero might be unrealistic and render you not alert enough to deal with things needing attention.

This script seems to be helpful to teach clients a natural way to decrease levels of tension, stress, and anxiety. I believe this phenomenon is related to something I learned from Dr. John Wolfe, who was chairman of the department of psychology at the University of Mississippi when I was in graduate school. A Yale graduate, Dr. Wolfe was part of the history of psychology, having taught chimpanzees at the Yerkes lab in the 1930s to work for tokens they could then put into an apparatus to get food. It was the first ever token economy. Years later, psychiatric hospitals started using token economies to reward patients, who could use their tokens to purchase items at the hospital store. The lesson from Dr. Wolfe I am referring to is as follows: You cannot unlearn a negative behavior. Instead, you can learn a new positive behavior that is incompatible with the old one you want to change.

In conclusion, this case reflects how mental conditions, such as anxiety, can undermine attempts to focus on peak performance in golf (or any other sport). In such situations, perhaps you need to deal with any mental and emotional issues first, and then you can focus on improving your game.

Case Five: The Child Golfer

This case involves a ten-year-old male with whom I was working while I wrote my 2011 book. He had been performing fairly well at golf, but his parents thought he could perhaps learn better concentration and focus. They were especially concerned about how down on himself he got when he played poorly or even after one bad shot. He would be filled with self-doubt and basically beat himself up. The case reminded me of a young soccer player I knew who would put himself in time-out if he felt he had played poorly or if his team lost.

Since the family traveled approximately two and a half hours each way for our sessions, we decided to always schedule double sessions. The techniques used were no different from those I use with adult golfers or young athletes from other sports.

He went to the US Kids Golf World Championship at Pinehurst Resort, North Carolina, in August 2010. We preplanned a long-distance telephone consult the evening before the competition; however, due to his busy practice schedule and other tournament activities, we were unable to speak until the following evening. When I asked about his first round, he said he had shot an 80 and was standing twenty-fifth to thirtieth of 140 competitors. He exclaimed, "I had a good mental game today! I had a new caddie, and he didn't make me get down or anything." He said he was twelve behind the first-place golfer and three or four behind number twenty (which was what he'd said he would like to accomplish—to be at least number twenty). I presented the following script to him by phone.

> I want you to put yourself into a self-hypnotic state, just as we practice in my office and as you have been practicing at home. Let me know when you are there. [He said, "Umm."] Okay, now concentrate on your breathing, slowing it down, just as when you are in a deep sleep ... Now count yourself down from ten to one, with each number making you more deeply relaxed ... Okay, now concentrate on what I am saying. Tomorrow you do not need to

try to make up the twelve shots to try to be number one. Focus on making up the three or four shots to be number twenty, your goal for the tournament ... If you happen to be having a great game and think you can do even better, then you can focus on passing more of the leaders.

I would like you to practice tonight. Ask your mom and dad to go out for a cup of coffee while you practice self-hypnosis in the hotel room. Tell them I said to do this. Then I want you to visualize each hole. All of the eighteen holes are the same ones you played today, right? [He answered, "Yes, sir."] So you are now familiar with the course, and you tell yourself, "I've already done this once, so I'll do better this time around."

If you had particular trouble with one hole, tell yourself, "Well, I have plenty of room for improvement, so I'll do better." [He responded, "Yes, sir."] Next, visualize each shot before you take it, and use the locking-in and flicking-out technique I taught you to lock in the good and get rid of any bad shots.

Remember to breathe deeply, just as when you are in the chair in my office or when you are practicing self-hypnosis at home ... Relax, and focus only on that next shot ... Does that make sense? [He responded, "Yes, sir."] Any questions? [He responded, "No, sir."] Great! I am looking forward to seeing you again after you get home.

When they returned to see me at my office, the parents and the young golfer indicated they were pleased with the results.

In summary, a number of different strategies and techniques can be used in golf, just as in other sports. A sound emotional base, along with learning to focus, concentrate, and block out distractions, is essential to achieve peak performance.

CHAPTER 3

Your Self-Hypnosis Training: Let's Begin

The following are techniques to get into a hypnotic relaxation state.

First Hypnotic Session
Induction and Deepening

We will start with a reverse arm levitation induction, followed by deep-breathing techniques and a deepening method involving the visual imagery of an elevator ride to a safe, comfortable room.

Reverse Arm Levitation

> I invite you to find yourself a comfortable position on a couch, chair, or bed; place one arm out in front of you with your elbow bent; and pick a spot on your hand that gets your attention ... Perhaps a ring, a fingernail, or a knuckle. Whatever gets your attention ... Now stare at that spot and nothing else ... We are creating tension in that arm and in your eyes ... The rest of your body will do what is natural or normal, and that is to relax ... It takes energy to be tense, so now you are placing the energy into your arm and your eyes ... The natural pull of gravity will cause that arm to feel heavier and heavier ... The natural response to staring in that

manner will be for the eyes to feel heavier and heavier, and they might even start tearing up ... You will feel the need to blink more frequently, and each time you blink, pay attention to your eyelids, as they will seem to get heavier and heavier. You will wish to close them ... but I invite you to keep staring at that spot until your hand touches all the way down ... to your leg, your lap, or the chair—wherever it winds up ... When it touches down, this is your signal to yourself that you are ready to let go of all tension and relax further all over.

The neat part about this technique is that when you can place the tension where you want to place it—in this case, in just the arm and the eyes—you are in charge of the tension ... You are in control of it, meaning you also have the ability to let it go whenever you choose ... You are in control ... You can hold on to that tension as long as you like, or you can let it go as soon as you like ... You're in charge of that ... As soon as it touches down, let go of all tension, and relax further all over.

Deep Breathing

Next, take a deep breath, and hold it ... Now exhale and relax ... Again, take a deep breath ... Now breathe out slowly and relax ... Again, take a deep breath ... Now relax.

Breathing is the key to relaxation ... One of the things we know about human behavior is that people are most relaxed when they are in a really deep sleep ... During this deep sleep state, people's breathing becomes slow and heavy, slow and deep ... By imitating this breathing style, you can become just as relaxed as you would be in a really deep sleep. So focus on your breathing … Breathe slow and heavy … Slow and deep.

As you breathe in, you might think the word *relax* … As you exhale, imagine any tension escaping from your body … Relax in … Tension out … Relax in … Tension out.

Deepening

The Elevator Imagery

Now, to get you more deeply relaxed, we are going to use a technique called visual imagery. Visual imagery is what we did when you imagined the beach scene. Some people refer to this as visualization. I sometimes call it getting a picture in your mind's eye, almost as if you have a screen behind your eyes, and the mind can see it. With the beach scene, you proved you are good at visual imagery.

Next, I invite you to imagine yourself on the tenth floor of a building. It could be a building you have been in before, or it could be one you have seen in a movie or on TV, but imagine there are ten floors. You are on the top floor, and you want to take an elevator ride all the way down to the bottom floor, the first floor. Each floor, as you go down, is going to symbolize or represent for you a deeper level of hypnotic relaxation. Use all of your senses. As you count down, I invite you to see yourself, feel yourself, and sense yourself going deeper with each number.

Let's start with the tenth floor. Imagine you are standing in front of the elevator doors. The doors open, and you step inside ... You turn around and face the front, and you see a control panel with ten buttons, one for each floor, plus a couple more that open and close the doors. Nod your head gently when you get a picture in your mind's eye of the control panel ... If you have difficulty, think about the last elevator you were in.

Now I want you to imagine pushing the button for the first floor, and nod when you have done so ... Good. You have pushed the button, and you are ready to start your descent. But first, notice that above the doors is a set of lights and numbers, a way of monitoring your trip. Now you have pushed the button and are ready to start your descent.

Go from floor ten down to nine ... Go deeper to eight. The counting is paced with each breath exhaled. This pacing should result in the slowing of your breathing as the counting is slowed ... You're at seven, going deeper. Every muscle and fiber in your body is relaxing further and deeper with each number as you count ... Six and deeper ... At five, you are halfway down, and with the remaining numbers, let go of all remaining tension, and relax very deeply ... Four ... Three and deeper ... Two ... All the way down to one, relaxing deeply.

When you get to the bottom floor, imagine the elevator doors opening. You step into a hallway or corridor and from there into a room ... A warm, safe, peaceful, comfortable room. It could be a room you have been in before. It might even be your favorite room. Or it could be one you've seen in a movie or maybe in a magazine. Let me tell you how I see the room, and then you can either adopt my model or create your own. I see it as warm, safe, peaceful, and tranquil. Perhaps there is thick carpet on the floor, along with a couch or an easy chair, the kind you sink down into

> *until you feel almost as if you are part of the furniture ... See yourself entering the room, however you see it in your mind's eye, and walk over to the couch or chair, or bed or pillows—whatever furnishings are there—and really settle in, sinking in. You're becoming so deeply relaxed it's hard to tell where your body stops and the furnishings beneath you begin. If you allow yourself, you can become that relaxed right here on this furniture. So deeply relaxed it's hard to tell where your body stops and the furniture beneath you begins ... Appreciate how relaxed you're becoming ... Appreciate how relaxed you've become ... In a state of perfect relaxation, you feel unwilling to move a single muscle in your body. And see how good it feels to know that you don't have to move a single muscle in your body.*

We may use this safe room to imagine a movie screen or giant TV screen on which we can later return to look at videos of how we want things to be in the future regarding performance (i.e., mental rehearsal).

Second Hypnotic Session

I prefer to use different induction and deepening techniques in subsequent sessions, including eye fixation, an eye-roll approach, and progressive relaxation (imagined, not via progressive relaxation exercises). I've done this by design so that when you're practicing on your own, you can pick and choose the techniques you like best. Different people prefer different methods.

> *Last time, I had you stare at a spot on your hand, thus creating tension in the arm and in the eyes. This time, I recommend you stare at a spot on the wall, something above your line of vision ... Do not lift your head; only gaze up so you are placing tension in the eyes ... So the first time, the tension was in your arm and in your eyes, but this time,*

it's specifically in the eyes. The only tension of which you are aware while the rest of the body relaxes is in your eyes. The rest of your body will do what comes naturally and normally, which is to relax. Remember, the body's natural response is relaxation ... It takes energy to be tense.

Again, as you place the tension where you want to—in this case, just in the eyes—you are in control of that tension. You are in charge of it, meaning you can let it go completely whenever you are ready.

As your eyes close, concentrate on your breathing, just as we did in session one. Remember, breathing is the key to relaxation. Breathe as you would in a deep sleep ... Slow and heavy ... Slow and deep, in with relaxation and out with tension ... Relax in. Tension out.

Next, to get you more deeply relaxed, we will again use visual imagery. In session one, we used the image of an elevator ride ... This time, imagine a staircase ... Perhaps a spiral staircase or a majestic stairwell like in an old mansion ... Each step as you go down is going to symbolize a deeper level of relaxation ... Go from step ten down to nine ... Nine down to eight ... At seven, every muscle and fiber in your body relaxes further and deeper ... Six ... At five, you are halfway down, and with the remaining numbers, you go deeper and deeper ... Four ... Three ... Two ... And one. At one, you're relaxing very deeply and feeling how good it feels to relax and not have to move a single muscle in your body.

Third Hypnotic Session

The next approach is one I especially like for a couple of reasons: the eye-roll technique. First, it is quick, and second, you can do it anywhere at any time, even in front of people, simply by covering your eyes. People might think you are just thinking or, at worst, maybe have a headache. No one will know you are doing a self-hypnosis technique. A golfer, for example, could perform this technique before or even during a round.

> *I invite you to roll your eyes so that you are looking up through your eyebrows or through the top of your head. This process causes tension very quickly in the eyes due to the severe angle at which you are looking, and you will wish to close your eyes. When you are ready, go ahead and close them comfortably and gently.*
>
> *Next, focus on your breathing once more, as described above, breathing as you would in a deep sleep, slow and heavy, slow and deep.*
>
> *Following the breathing exercise, you can use either of the two visual images given above, the elevator or the staircase, or perhaps an escalator or a gently sloping hill, as long as each number symbolizes a deeper level of hypnotic relaxation.*

Subsequent Sessions

After the first three sessions, as you become more experienced in my approach, I invite you to use what I refer to as "flex induction," during which you choose which of the previous induction and deepening techniques seem most useful for you. I tell clients,

You have been practicing a variety of induction techniques on your own. Some clients prefer some methods, and others prefer others. Now put yourself into a hypnotic state using whichever technique you like best.

I have come to realize that for some clients, just sitting in a recliner becomes a conditioned stimulus to induce hypnosis. After a while, some clients just close their eyes and find they can go under quickly.

The Importance of Personalization of Your Approach

A while after writing my first hypnosis book, I came across an article I had published years earlier (Tramontana 1983). That case study, which focused on the importance of subject bias in hypnosis with children, reinforces the philosophy of letting my client (you) choose the induction from a number of options learned. The subject in that case was a six-year-old thumb sucker. I noted in the study that although I routinely questioned adults and adolescent clients regarding their knowledge of hypnosis, I entered into only a laconic and perhaps perfunctory discussion with the child because of his young age.

Over a period of several weeks, I attempted to induce hypnosis using several of my usual techniques. Although the subject cooperated slightly and to varying degrees, his distractibility resulted in instances of his interrupting to ask questions, opening his eyes to check on the therapist, and so on. Finally, after I made several failed attempts to get him into a hypnotic state, he told me, "You aren't doing it right." He had seen someone hypnotized on his favorite TV program, *Knight Rider*. He explained that in the show, the hypnotist used a swinging watch.

I improvised by tying the cord of a tape recorder to my stopwatch to produce a pendulum effect. Once I did it "the right way" according to the subject, a moderately deep hypnotic state resulted.

While the athletes I see for sports hypnosis are more sophisticated and informed than was that young child, I sometimes tell this story to let athletes know why I think it is important to allow them to choose techniques, especially for self-hypnotic work.

At some point, especially when I want you to look into the future (future projection), I might have you count forward from one to ten and imagine you're on an escalator riding up into the clouds, with each number taking you to a higher level of relaxation, where you can see things from a better perspective and be above the humdrum of daily living. Again, after you become experienced in my deepening techniques, I will say the same words I use with the induction:

> *You have been practicing a number of different deepening techniques, so you can pick whichever one you like best and allow yourself to go deeper now. Continue until you have completed the deepening technique in your mind.*

My methods begin in a formalized way but evolve into a consideration of your needs and preferences. This approach continues to develop by my asking you, "What would you like [or what do you feel you need] to work on today in hypnosis?"

The sessions typically evolve from structured, detailed approaches to shorter, less detailed, and more flexible ones. I prefer the reverse arm levitation induction in the first hypnotic session because this approach is slower and more dramatic than some of the other techniques. While I describe to you what you likely feel in your arm and in your eyes, you actually feel the natural physiological responses of your arm and eyes getting heavier. The ensuing more flexible and less detailed approaches are especially important for athletes since, early on, you will be instructed in quick, open-eyed (alert) hypnosis for your competition. While you can practice with eyes closed at home, on the day of the competition and during the match, you certainly will be wide awake—in fact, to a heightened level of awareness.

The Practice Effect and Generalization Effect

You will discover how much easier it becomes over time to enter a trance and how the skill generalizes to other areas of your life. The following suggestions are geared toward teaching you to do so.

> *With your eyes closed, relax, and concentrate on my words. I'm going to tell you some interesting things about hypnosis. You don't have to concentrate on what I am saying, because your subconscious will pick it up anyway. I'm going to tell you about two effects. The first one I call the "practice effect." As with most other behaviors, just as in your physical practice of your game, the more you practice, the better your performances get. So let me suggest to you that anytime you want to go into a hypnotic state, you will go into hypnosis more quickly and more deeply.*

I typically repeat the suggestion three times and say, "Three is the magic number that locks it in."

> *With practice, you will get better at putting yourself into a hypnotic state more quickly and more deeply. The key word here is the word want: when you want to go into hypnosis. No one can put you into a hypnotic state against your will, and you will never spontaneously go into a hypnotic state—for example, while operating machinery or driving a car. You will do so only when you want to, only when it is to your advantage to do so.*

The second effect I call "the generalization effect."

This effect is really an ego-strengthening approach, which I find to be especially important to athletes.

> *The generalization effect refers to the fact that regardless of why you are learning hypnosis, whether to improve sports performance, stop smoking, lose weight, lower subjective levels of pain, decrease stress, overcome addictions, or improve study habits—there are many applications of hypnosis—the one common denominator or common fringe benefit, as I call it, is that you learn to be calm and more relaxed. That is what hypnosis is all about: learning to be calmer and more relaxed ... As you learn to be calmer and more relaxed, your functioning becomes more efficient and effective. As your functioning becomes more efficient and effective, your self-confidence improves, which leads to greater calm and more relaxation, even more efficiency and effectiveness, and even more self-confidence.*

Efficiency and Effectiveness

The primary goal of our hypnotic work is to reinforce a positive or optimistic forecast for success in your golf game. Let me explain.

> *Many people—perhaps most people—expend too much emotional energy, much more than particular situations call for. This is what I call "spinning your wheels emotionally." Think of a car stuck in a mudhole. You rev or race the engine, and the wheels spin, but you don't go anywhere, because you have no traction. As you learn to be calmer and more relaxed, you will engage in less of that emotional wheel-spinning, which will lead your functioning to become more efficient and effective. As you learn to function more efficiently and effectively, your self-confidence will improve, which will lead to even more calm, relaxation, efficiency, effectiveness, self-confidence, and so on in a cycle of progress that grows, deepens, strengthens, and reinforces itself.*

I like to refer to this cycle of progress as the snowball effect: when a little ball of snow rolls down a hill, it gets larger and larger as it gathers more and more snow. The end result of this cycle of progress is that you will have a better self-image, a better self-concept, and greater feelings of self-esteem. In other words, you will like yourself better, and you will be convinced you can accomplish not only specific day-to-day tasks but just about anything, within reason, that you set your mind to—and you will be able to do so calmly, effectively, efficiently, and with confidence.

Trance Ratification

After the generalization effect, I will focus on trance ratification, which is vitally important in creating a sense of expectancy for you that hypnosis will work. This experience will provide you with a convincer, ratifying for you that you have entered into an altered state of consciousness. Glove anesthesia is one ratification technique. I used to use glove anesthesia with pain patients to demonstrate to them their ability to lower subjective pain, but I stopped because of negative reactions to the idea of being pricked with a sharp object. That technique involves telling the client,

> *In just a moment, I'm going to stick your hand with a sharp object, and you will be amazed that you feel a slight pressure but no pain.*

I never used this technique with athletes unless pain from an injury was impeding performance in competition or preventing it completely. Now I might describe the technique to clients but do not actually use it. I use the following three ratification techniques:

> *Earlier, I told you that you did not have to concentrate—that your subconscious would understand anyway. Now,*

however, I am going to ask you to do just the opposite: I want you to concentrate intently on what I am saying. I want you to use the power of your creative mind, your imagination, to imagine some things as I describe them to you.

The first thing I want you to imagine is that your eyes are glued closed. They are glued shut, as if you accidentally got some superglue on the lids or lashes and cannot open them ... As you imagine your eyelids tightly glued shut, let the muscles in your eyes try to open them as your mind tells you that you cannot open them because they are glued shut ... Notice the resistance. [Rarely has a client opened his or her eyes.] Mind over matter. Mind over body.

Now stop trying to open them. Imagine the glue has worn off—but you decide to keep them closed anyway, until later, when I tell you to open them.

Now, just as we did with the muscle testing, I want you to place one arm out in front of you at about shoulder height. Make it very rigid ... That's right ... Make a fist, and make the arm very rigid, just like a bar of steel—an unbendable bar of steel. You might even create a picture in your mind's eye of a bar of steel there instead of an arm, tight and taut and unbendable. Now, as your mind tells you that is an unbendable bar of steel instead of an arm, let the muscles of the arm try to bend it. Notice the resistance there ... Very good.

Next, imagine that the arm is no longer a bar of steel. Instead, it is like a wet, floppy dishcloth. Limp and loose like a dishcloth falling to the kitchen floor.

As expected, the arm will typically flop down beside you. In fact, a person's response to this exercise is one of the factors I consider when determining his or her hypnotizability or depth of trance. If one gently lowers the arm, he or she might just be going along with what he or she thinks I expect. If the arm drops like a dishcloth, the response indicates the person is truly in, or entering into, a hypnotic state. Then, depending on the specific application, the appropriate suggestions follow.

The Beach Scene

Since so much of the first session is spent on goal-setting and orientation to hypnosis, with a golfer looking to improve his or her game, there is not much time left for me to give him or her suggestions regarding that particular sport. But because I want the person to leave the first session with something positive and encouraging to remember, I tell him or her to concentrate on these words:

> *Now let's focus on getting you even more deeply relaxed. To do this, we are going to have you imagine some relaxing scenes. First, I want you to imagine a beach scene or, if not a beach, perhaps the ocean. You could be on the sand or on grass. I want you to imagine yourself sitting on a beach towel or blanket or in a recliner of some sort, enjoying the weather and the scenery. You might imagine it is a beautiful spring or summer day. You feel the warm sunlight on your skin, and there is a nice breeze coming off the water.*

> *Enjoying the weather and the scenery, you watch some sailboats off in the distance. It is a fairly calm day, and you notice how effortlessly the boats seem to move through the water, pushed by the gentle breeze. There might be some seagulls flying nearby, near the water's edge, and you notice they too seem to glide effortlessly on the wind currents. Perhaps there is a ship on the horizon ... Although we know it takes a lot of power to propel a ship, the efficient*

use of power causes a seeming effortlessness ... Maybe a jet plane flies across the sky ... It too takes a tremendous amount of power. The efficient use of power, however, causes a seeming effortlessness.

These are your key words: efficient and effortless.

The Woods Scene

Let us now go to a second scene. Imagine a woods scene, perhaps a state park setting. Imagine a beautiful fall morning. There is nice sunlight, but you feel the certain cool crispness in the air that you get on a beautiful fall morning. You are walking down a path in the woods, enjoying the weather and the scenery. The leaves are turning colors; birds are chirping; and you are enjoying the sights, sounds, and smells of the forest.

As you continue walking along the path, you notice an area ahead in which there are no trees. You get closer and see the reason there are no trees: there is a body of water running through, like a narrow river or wide stream. You notice how effortlessly the water seems to flow, clean and clear ... It is so crystal clear and clean you can see your reflection in the water. You might even see a reflection of yourself at a younger age, at some earlier time when everything seemed easier. Perhaps you were more happy-go-lucky and more carefree.

You notice how steadily the water flows—how predictably, reliably, efficiently, and effortlessly ... There are those key words again: efficient and effortless.

There might be some rocks and pebbles near the water's edge, where the water is only an inch or two deep, and you notice how the water goes over and around the rocks and pebbles. Perhaps there are some boulders out in the middle, and you notice how there too the water just goes over or around and continues its path effortlessly.

You continue to walk down the bank of the river or stream and come upon a walking bridge, the kind you might see in a state park. It is a wooden bridge with curved handrails—some people call them footbridges. You decide you want to cross over to the other side, so you step up onto the bridge and begin to walk across.

As you get halfway across, you notice that something below has gone awry. The water below is not as clean and clear anymore. It is muddy and dirty and backing up, not flowing smoothly anymore. As you look more closely, you see what has happened: some logs floating down the body of water got lodged under the bridge, causing a logjam. As you investigate more closely, you see that one log is bigger than the rest. This log is the main problem. It got wedged under the bridge, causing the others to back up behind it. I want you to concentrate on that big log ... See if something is written on that log ... Written, engraved, or inscribed on that log. It could be a word ... It might even be a name. It could be a sentence or maybe a full paragraph.

Some people see something, and some do not, but regardless of whether or not they do, what is most important is the next step.

I invite you to make a commitment to take matters into your own hands to free up the problem, to remedy the problem ... You cross over to the other side, and you find a board or a pipe or a tree limb—something you can use as a lever ... Then you set about the task of freeing up the logjam. Whether it involves leaning over from the bridge, leaning out from the bank, or even wading into the water, you use the board, pipe, or tree limb as a lever to pry loose the big log. To your surprise, with a little effort, it begins to loosen up, and after it loosens, it floats freely again, passing under the bridge. The other logs then follow suit.

You go back up onto the bridge and watch as the logs float off into the distance. The farther away they get, the smaller they seem, until they are so far away they are like tiny specks in the distance. Finally, they round a bend, and you do not see them at all anymore; you know they still exist somewhere, but they are no longer in your field of experience.

You look back down into the water, and it is once again flowing smoothly, cleanly, reliably, and predictably. You are proud you took the necessary action to free up the jam. You see your reflection again, but this time at your present age, in the here and now, and you see yourself looking much happier, like the younger person you saw in the beginning, free from worry ... You might even smile at yourself as you take pride in the fact that you took matters into your own hands to rectify and remedy the problem.

Now, as you may or may not have already figured out, this is a metaphor filled with symbolism. The body of water symbolizes one's path through life, which is why we showed you at an early age, clean and clear and free. The little rocks and pebbles symbolize minor setbacks and frustrations, and of course, the boulders represent bigger problems. The logjam represents a major blockage, perhaps what is blocking you from being your best self. Some people don't see anything written on the log, but others see something

> *written on the log that might give them a clue as to what their blockage might be. Did you see anything written on the log? Some people see a name—perhaps even their own name, suggesting they are their own biggest problem—but the key is the decision to take matters into your own hands to free up the logjam. This action could be symbolic of your buying this book and practicing these techniques. Perhaps hypnosis is the lever, board, pipe, or tree limb to help pry loose whatever has been blocking you.*
>
> *In any event, once the main log is loosened, life begins to flow more smoothly again, and as you look down now from the bridge, you see the water again as clear, clean, and flowing. You might see your reflection again but this time in the present time, and you might even be smiling, proud that you took matters into your own hands to remedy the problem.*

This logjam imagery is effective in helping to release blocks, which some golfers refer to as yips. The logs, and especially the big log, might be directly related to what is limiting your success.

In subsequent sessions, you can utilize other deepening techniques, such as imagining an escalator ride or descending a gently sloping hill down to a beautiful valley, river, or body of water.

As I stated earlier, after several sessions, you might want to count forward from one to ten while taking an imaginary trip up into the clouds. Some clients say they prefer this approach to counting down. I say, "From this vantage point, you see things more clearly than you do from ground level." I sometimes use this technique for creating a time continuum, as follows:

> *You can look to the left into the past (age regression) or to the right into the future (future projection or rehearsing success). Changing techniques and being flexible will help you increase your repertoire of techniques you can use in doing your own self-hypnotic work.*

CHAPTER 4

Additional Techniques

Whether you think you can or think you can't, you're right.

—Henry Ford

I use the term *techniques,* which might also be considered *therapeutic suggestions*. In fact, I often use the terms interchangeably.

After you determine your situation, problems, and goals, self-hypnosis training begins. First, if you were in my office, I would use the muscle-testing technique described in chapter 2 to show you how important the mental aspect of your game is. You can use this technique by yourself. Then I would give the test of hypnotic suggestibility in chapter 2, featuring the children on the beach with their sand buckets. Just as with other hypnotic clients, I would utilize the induction and deepening techniques, along with other approaches described in chapter 2.

I use many of the suggestions offered by Dr. Bob Rotella, the famous sports psychologist, who has written several books about golf. In his foreword to Dr. Bob's book *Golf Is Not a Game of Perfect*, Tom Kite talks about meeting Doc at the 1984 Doral Open while in a phase when nothing was going right. Doc merely refreshed his memory about the great thoughts he usually had when he played his best, and he went out and won the tournament, beating none other than Jack Nicklaus.

Once you are in a hypnotic state, I recommend you focus on the following suggestions. These suggestions are consistent with those given conversationally by Dr. Rotella but here are given hypnotically instead:

Concentrate on the following: Rotella says that golfing potential depends primarily on a player's attitude, how well he or she plays with the wedges and the putter, and how well he or she thinks. He tells players to think about their hottest streak. That hot streak represents a player's true level of ability. When in it, the golfer is trusting of his or her abilities and plays at his or her true level, not over his or her head but at maximum capacity, without self-doubt. He tells players, "During your hot streak, you probably were not thinking about the mechanics of your swing. You weren't getting in your own way from a mental standpoint. You trusted your mechanics. You are not listening to me to improve your mechanics; you already know what you are supposed to do, and if work needs to be done on your mechanics, perhaps you need to talk to a golf coach about this. Think about your mental state during hot streaks, and replicate that state of mind."

Before taking any shot, you should pick out the smallest possible target; focus on that target and nothing else; and, especially, pay no attention to the hazards. Know where they are, but focus on your target. If you focus on the hazard, even though it is a focus on something you want to avoid, guess where you are likely to wind up. It is almost like programming in a negative expectancy.

Preshot Routine

A sound preshot routine is essential for consistency. If you watch elite golfers, you will notice they all follow a set preshot routine. This routine involves not only physical movements but also a set of mental thoughts. Some say the preshot routine is a major part of the results. It ensures you set up properly mentally as well as physically. It helps to block out distractions. This is what our work together will help you to accomplish.

As I said earlier, your golf coach is the one to look to for mechanics. Our work together is to help you concentrate, block out distractions, focus, and accomplish the results you desire by using the self-hypnotic techniques in this book.

> *During this preshot state, assess the shot, pick the club, focus on the target, adjust for the lie and stance variations, and block out everything else. Now visualize the shot, and see the ball going exactly where you choose for it to go.*
>
> *Next, I am going to teach you a kinetic signaling technique to get you just as relaxed as you are in your relaxing place. As you continue to relax and concentrate in this manner, I want you to touch two fingers together, such as your thumb and index finger or your thumb and middle finger … Good … This is going to be your kinesthetic signal to remind your mind and body to get just as relaxed and to focus just as much as in this moment of relaxation. Anytime you are practicing, competing, or doing anything that would benefit from increasing your relaxation and focus, I want you to touch two fingers together, and you will get just as relaxed and focused as you are right now. You can do so throughout your competition, especially during breaks and between shots.*
>
> *You might also modify this technique for immediate preshot use. For example, as you relax and focus in this manner, I want you to now imagine your grip on the club just before the shot. Imagine how it feels … With this image in mind, associate this current feeling of relaxed focus with the feel of the grip, and when you grip your club before your shot, this will be your signal to get just as relaxed and focused as you are right now.*

I want to teach you a method for locking in good shots and discarding bad ones. After a good shot, I want you to lock it in. You might do a clutching movement, as baseball player Kirk Gibson did when he hit the home run that won the first game of the World Series in 1988. [While younger athletes perhaps were not even born then, some of my older clients remember the scene well.] Whether you use this movement or not, let me describe the scenario: In the 1988 World Series, the Los Angeles Dodgers were underdogs to the heavily favored Oakland Athletics, who had won many more games that year. In the game, after hitting the winning home run, as he headed to first and rounded the bases, Gibson kept making a clutching, pumping motion with his right arm. That event precipitated an inspired series in which the Dodgers went on to win in five games. Some people refer to such motions as muscle memory.

I invite you, after a good shot, to lock it in … You don't have to be as dramatic as Gibson … Perhaps you just clench your fist … Just find a signal to lock it in. But then forget about it … You do not want to continue thinking about a past shot, even a good shot, as it might interfere with preparation for the next.

In a case in which the shot is less than you are satisfied with, I want you to make a gesture that symbolizes getting rid of it. I learned this from an old spiritual teacher regarding healing touch: get rid of any negativity by shaking out your hand. While in competition, you can do this subtly if you choose.

The World-Class Visualizer

Another metaphor I find produces good results is one I call the "world-class visualizer."

I want you to imagine that you have a secret garden ... It could be behind your home, or it could be somewhere totally different ... I invite you to imagine entering that garden. Look around, and then I would like for you to describe everything you see.

Take a few minutes ... Many people describe seeing flowers, trees, perhaps colors and textures, paths through the garden, and perhaps a pond ... Very good!

Now I want you to imagine that you see the garden through the eyes of and with the brain of a world-class visualizer. Perhaps a famous artist or an inventor. Einstein was said to be a world-class visualizer ... Things look different through his or her eyes and with his or her brain, don't they?

You have been seeing your golf game for so long through your own eyes and with your own brain ... Now I want you to imagine seeing it through the eyes of and with the brain of a world-class golfer, perhaps someone you admire and would like to emulate ... Someone who is similar enough to you in other ways that you might be able to adopt his or her techniques to work for you ... Someone who knows exactly how to counsel you regarding what will work for you in terms of your game, from the mechanics of your swing to the mental side of golf ... Do you see, feel, sense, or know anything different from this expert's perspective?

What is different? What comes to you that might be changed to improve your performance? ... Now I want you to adopt this perspective or viewpoint as your own ... After all, it is yours because it came from your own creative mind. Your unconscious mind knows what to do and how to do it!

Space Travel Meditation

This method is a problem-solving technique that can be used in a wide variety of life situations. It is similar to the world-class visualizer approach in that it is a method of channeling information from your subconscious mind to your conscious mind through an imagined all-wise being.

> *Concentrate on what I am saying: I invite you to imagine that you are going to take a trip ... You know, travel can be very educational ... People who are well-traveled are often considered to be wise, and in fact, that is why schools take children on field trips; isn't it just so they can be exposed to more of the world around them and how it works. So I invite you to imagine that we are going to take a fantasy trip into outer space.*
>
> *First, I want you to imagine looking at your home from ground level ... After you have that image in mind, next, imagine looking down on your home from above, as you might see it from a helicopter or hot air balloon ... Things look different when you're looking down from above ... If you have ever been on the roof of your home, you likely remember how things looked different from that vantage point.*
>
> *Now you are so high you can see the entire area in which you live, as you might see it from a small plane ... Now you see the whole city as you might see it from a jetliner ... Now you see the entire region of the country and, as you get higher and higher, the United States, the North American continent, and, finally, planet Earth ... Earth looks the way you might see it from a spaceship or satellite.*

Now imagine yourself in outer space, and you can travel anywhere you want out there—another planet or a star. Definitely not Earth. The only restriction is that it must be a place that is positive or at least neutral—no places that are negative, evil, or scary ... During at least one of your stops, you are going to meet an all-wise being ... He or she or it can be humanlike or can be very different, but imagine this being has all the wisdom of the universe, all the wisdom of the cosmos available, and is willing to share that wisdom with you ... All you need to do is ask the questions, and the answers will come.

Most people will ask questions about issues for which they are seeing me. For example, "What is the problem blocking me from performing at my highest level?" ... The next obvious question would then be "What do I need to do differently?" ... Continue your journey ... After some time, process to yourself where you went, whom you met, what questions you asked, and what answers came to you, and describe to yourself what you learned.

The world-class traveler and space travel metaphors highlight the fact that we all have much more wisdom, often in our unconscious or subconscious mind (I use the two terms interchangeably), than we realize. That is why, for example, when we attend a continuing education conference to learn something new, we might leave thinking, *I knew that!* We often know much more than we realize we know. These two metaphors are a technique to channel information from your unconscious mind to your conscious mind through the world-class visualizer or all-wise inner being.

Time-Continuum Future Success Technique

After a number of sessions using the deepening techniques involving counting backward, I invite you to change it up a little as follows:

This time, instead of counting backward, count forward from one to ten, and this time, imagine a trip up into the clouds ... Perhaps an escalator ride up to a platform in the clouds ... Now, this is a fantasy, of course, but fantasies can be very relaxing.

After counting up to ten, imagine a platform in the clouds ... Soft, fleecy white clouds are floating all around you ... You are curious about these clouds ... You wonder if they will support you ... You decide to experiment ... You set one foot on a cloud ... To your pleasant surprise, the cloud does support you ... So you step out onto the cloud and sit down or maybe even lie down with your head propped up by one elbow and arm, luxuriating in your soft, fleecy, floating white cloud ... From that vantage point up in the clouds, you can see the world going on below. You see people going about their daily routines ... You can even see yourself going through your day's activities ... You can also imagine a continuum of time ... Directly beneath you is the present ... Off to the left is the past ... The near left is the recent past, and the far left is the distant past ... If you're investigating possible past events that might have led to your sabotaging yourself, this technique could be a form of age regression, but it can also be a means of age progression or future projection ... Off to the right is the future ... The near right is the near future, and the far right is the distant future ... We can use this technique to look into the future ... Now, we can't necessarily predict the future, unless, of course, we are clairvoyant ... But we can project how we would like it to be.

> *I invite you to spend some time projecting future success ... Imagine everything working out just the way you would want it to work out if you were writing the script for a movie or a play.*

Confidence-Building Technique

Next, continue with the following (this can be done in a separate session from the earlier ones):

> *As you now go deeper into relaxation, you can begin to realize that with every positive experience, you will grow more and more confident, increasing your feelings of self-worth ... More and more, you come to realize that only positive thoughts are of any value to you, and negative thoughts can be discarded as having no value ... But you also know that an error or mistake or loss is only an opportunity to do it differently next time—to improve and to refine ... Even champion athletes are never perfect all of the time.*
>
> As the story goes, Thomas Edison was on his thousandth trial of inventing the electric lightbulb, when a friend said, "Thomas, I can't believe you don't just give up. I would hate to have to admit that I failed nine hundred ninety-nine times."
>
> Thomas reportedly responded, "Oh, I haven't failed at all. I have just discovered nine hundred ninety-nine ways *not* to invent the electric lightbulb."
>
> You have all the confidence you need to carry you through your plan to practice until you become better and better, more and more competitive, until you

achieve your maximum potential … Only when you have reached your maximum potential and perform to your fullest, greatest potential can you think about getting even better and raising the bar, so to speak, on a higher maximum potential … You are calm and relaxed, confident in your ability to learn, to improve, to excel.

In summary, there are a number of different strategies and techniques you can use to strengthen your mental game. Typically, the goal is not reinventing the wheel, so to speak, but, rather, presenting and reinforcing the suggestions given by Rotella (1995, 1996, 2004) and others who write about techniques to improve golf scores, although they do so only conversationally, while we are using self-hypnosis training as a means to reinforce and perhaps even lock in these concepts.

CHAPTER 5

More on the Importance of Self-Hypnosis Practice

To reinforce the importance of continuing your self-practice, I am including a story about an eight-year-old African American girl with a skin disorder. You might wonder what this has to do with golf or sports in general or any performance area. Well, it does not apply to performance specifically. It is about the importance of self-hypnotic work.

This beautiful little child's skin on her legs and arms looked like rubber. She had a bad case of eczema. She would scratch her arms and legs raw and then pick at the scabs, which would get infected. She spent a lot of time in the emergency room, especially during warm weather. The girl's mom called and asked if hypnosis could help. She said the pediatrician had shot down the idea. I informed her I had never used hypnosis for that condition but could certainly teach the child to relax and perhaps be less reactive and more in control.

The girl was a good hypnotic subject. I used a metaphor about pets. I asked if she had any, and she said she had two dogs and three cats, all of which were outside pets. "Well, I guess there is a fence to keep in the dogs," I said, and she affirmed that. "But the cats can climb fences and get out, right?" I said, and she nodded. "So what if you stopped feeding those cats? What do you think they would do?"

She said, "Um, they would go live somewhere else."

I said, "So when you scratch the itch, you are feeding the itch. But just like those cats, if you don't feed the itches, they will go away."

Well, guess what? She stopped scratching, and her skin began clearing up.

The mom reported that she took the child to the pediatrician for a regular well-child visit, and when she told him the hypnosis was proving to be effective, he again pooh-poohed the idea by saying, "Oh, well, it has been cool weather. Let's see what happens when it gets warmer." I suspect the doubter said it in front of the child. Doctors sometimes inadvertently give negative suggestions.

The child continued improving and, by late spring, was wearing shorts and sleeveless shirts, which she would not do when she thought her skin looked bad. Then came the first week in May, when I took my annual trip with my New Orleans buddies to Louisville for the Kentucky Derby. I informed the child I wouldn't see her for two weeks.

When I returned, the mother asked to speak with me for a minute first. She said, "My daughter was playing outside. It was a particularly hot day for early May, and she got a rash on the inside of her thigh. That is how it often starts." She said her daughter ran inside and told her, "Mommy, I need to see Dr. T." The mother reminded the girl that I was out of town and couldn't see her that week but asked if she wanted to go see the pediatrician. The child said, "No, he can't help me! Only Dr. T. can help me."

What happened next is the beautiful part of the story. The mother said, "Well, honey, why don't you go in your room and pretend you are talking to Dr. T.? Then do what he would tell you to do."

The child did, and she reportedly came out of her room about fifteen minutes later and announced, "I'm fine!" Then she proceeded to go back out and play—no rash and no itching.

I believe this eight-year-old girl's case reinforces just how important and powerful self-hypnotic work is. When you engage in negative thoughts, you enter a slippery slope of negativity. Replacing that negativity with positive self-talk changes the situation dramatically.

To Begin with Your Self-Hypnosis

At the end of the first hypnotic session, remember the four-step self-hypnosis approach. You were given the instructions for eye fixation, as described above in the second session:

> **Step 1.** In the first session you stared at a spot on your hand, localizing the tension in both your eyes and your arm. Now, however, just stare at a spot on the wall, localizing the tension just in the eyes. I invite you to do this on your own schedule. Stare at that spot, and when you decide to let go of the tension, close your eyes, and relax further all over. This is step one: creating the tension, and then letting it go.
>
> **Step 2.** Next comes deep breathing, as described above. Unless people have breathing problems, they tend to take breathing for granted, but if you spend two or three minutes focusing on your breathing, breathing slowly and deeply, it is like getting into your own mind and blocking out distractions. In the mindfulness meditation techniques done by monks, breathing is the key—just breathing and thinking of nothing.
>
> **Step 3.** Count down from ten to one, as described earlier, using whatever imagery feels comfortable.
>
> **Step 4.** Go to a relaxing place. I earlier mentioned two scenes: the beach scene and the woods scene. This works best if you have any memories of profoundly relaxing imagery you've experienced in real life. For example, one client said he was camping in the mountains and watching some eagles soar (eagles soaring might be a great metaphor for golfers), which was relaxing. Another client said that while visiting her girlfriend in Memphis

during the springtime, she slept upstairs in the guest bedroom with the windows wide open and awakened the next morning to the sound of a boy across the street playing a banjo. She said she felt almost as if she'd died and gone to heaven. People often refer to these relaxing scenes as going to their "safe place."

Once you're in your safe place, the time of day determines what you do next. If it is bedtime, suggest to yourself, "I am going to fall into a deep and restful sleep and not awaken until the desired time." If it is during the day, you will likely have other responsibilities, so tell yourself, "I will continue to relax for X minutes," whether it be thirty minutes, five minutes, or just one minute, depending on how much time you have available to relax. Tell yourself, "After that time, I will open my eyes, feeling wide awake, relaxed, refreshed, calm, confident, and alert."

How many times per day I recommend practicing self-hypnosis depends on the situation on which you are focused. With some clinical clients, I recommend practicing twice a day, but I find that athletes are so used to repetitions in their physical practice that they can be instructed to use self-hypnotic techniques many times a day. One technique is to teach going in and out of hypnosis during each TV commercial. Golfers, even if not regular watchers of various TV programs, typically watch golf or other sports on TV. This method also teaches you to move in and out of hypnosis quickly, which is often beneficial for your sports performance. I typically recommend that athletes practice self-hypnosis several times a day.

Another difference in working with athletes is that I almost always make a recording for their home practice. With other clinical applications of hypnosis, I typically only record a session if the client reports having trouble getting into the hypnotic state when practicing at home. With athletes, I typically do one unless they tell me they do not need or want the recording (which might make me question motivational levels). However, when I give a client a recording, I say, "With practice, you will depend less and less on the recording, because of course, you will not have access to this equipment during your competition." Since you, the reader, are not working directly with me in an office setting, if you choose, you can make your own recording using the scripts given above.

One theory maintains that some stress might relate to alertness. For example, if you are too relaxed, you might not be able to perform at peak levels. Some have written that peak performance is just below the point where anxiety begins. I learned something important from Dr. John Wolfe, who, as mentioned previously, worked at the Yerkes Laboratories of Primate Biology during the 1930s and taught chimps to work for tokens they could then use to secure food. Some years later, he became chairman of the psychology department at the University of Mississippi, where I attended graduate school. He taught that you can never unlearn a negative behavior; instead, you learn a new behavior that is incompatible with the old behavior. In working with athletes who have developed bad habits that hurt their performance, this is a particularly important point.

Alert and Open-Eye Hypnosis

With athletic competition, because you cannot compete with your eyes closed, the alert or open-eye trance is of particular benefit.

When you practice at home, just as in a clinical office, you will have your eyes closed, but you also can use techniques to get into a trance state with your eyes open and fully alert. After all, you cannot compete any other way! There are many good examples of open-eyed trances in our daily living. For example, have you ever been so focused on a TV show, book, or computer game that when someone came into the room and spoke to you, you really didn't comprehend what the person was saying? You were so focused on the show, book, or game that you kind of blocked the person out. Or perhaps, if you are old enough to drive, you have driven somewhere—to work, school, a social function, or maybe a practice or competition—and gotten there safely but not remembered the trip, including whether you stopped for traffic lights and so on. You were probably driving safely, but you were so focused on whatever you were thinking that you blotted out much of the drive. These are examples of open-eyed hypnosis, or what I sometimes call "mini-trances."

My technique regarding open-eyed hypnosis is somewhat different from those described by some other hypnosis practitioners, because I start with closed eyes and then incorporate open-eyed hypnosis, as described below.

You have been practicing hypnosis with your eyes closed in order to block out distractions, but of course, you must have your eyes wide open and be totally alert when practicing or competing, so this is what you are to do: before a practice or competition, put yourself into hypnosis using the quickest and most effective way that works for you, and give yourself a posthypnotic suggestion. The suggestion will depend on when you are performing the hypnotic technique (we will talk about a plan for you to use the technique at various times), as follows:

- If you are doing it immediately before the event: "I am going to open my eyes and be wide awake, alert, rested, energetic, and totally focused, just as focused as when my eyes were closed, focusing totally and only on the task at hand."
- If you are doing it the night before or morning of: "In X hours [or minutes], I am going to open my eyes and be wide awake, alert, rested, energetic, and totally focused, just as focused as when my eyes were closed, focusing totally and only on the task at hand."

CHAPTER 6

General Hypnotic and Therapeutic Approaches

I will now introduce some clinical approaches for readers who have come this far in the book but are still having problems with concentration, focus, or negative self-talk and are seeing a negative effect on their game. Often, such problems are related to low self-esteem, self-sabotage, or some other emotional reason. The clinical approaches I'll discuss include uncovering, reframing, and other cognitive behavioral techniques.

Uncovering

If you are self-sabotaging, I recommend uncovering work. In such cases, I recommend you see a hypnotherapist in addition to reading this book. Prior to your visiting a hypnotherapist to work with you on uncovering techniques, the following story might demonstrate the power of this approach.

Years ago, when I was on rotation to do psychological testing at an adolescent psychiatric hospital, I was called to see a sixteen-year-old girl admitted to the unit. The nurse told me when I arrived, "This kid feels like she doesn't fit in, and she really doesn't. The other kids don't like her." She didn't add, "And we don't like her," but that was the impression I got. But I liked her. She was a pretty girl, but of course, she thought she was ugly.

A few days after completing the examination, I received a call from the unit nurse. She said, "Dr. T., you are the only one who seemed to connect with this kid. Would you like to follow her on an outpatient basis when she is discharged?"

I replied, "Yes, but since I'm there a couple of days a week anyway, how about I start seeing her as an inpatient and then later at my outpatient office after discharge?" The hospital staff agreed.

In our first inpatient treatment session, I talked with her about her feeling of never fitting in. She admitted she felt that way but did not know from where the feeling originated. It was just always there. I talked with her about doing hypnosis (if her mom agreed) but noted it was too noisy there, with kids making noise in the hallways, the overhead intercom speakers, and so forth, but I said we could do it when she came to my office.

In our first outpatient session, I introduced hypnosis. She entered a hypnotic state easily. I had her imagine watching a movie of her life and told her as I counted backward from five to one that the film would rewind and that when we got to one, a picture would come into focus on the screen that would tell us about a significant experience in her past related to the problems she had in the present with not fitting in. When I got to one, she told a story that had occurred when she was three years old. She said she had just gotten out of the bathtub, so she had no clothes on, and she was playing on the floor with her dolls. Her mother entered the room and severely berated her. She told her what a nasty, naughty little girl she was and said, "Shame on you—naked!"

Tears ran down the child's face as she described the scene. I remember thinking, *I'll bet that wasn't the first time something like that occurred.*

I told her I was going to count backward again, and that time, when I got to one, I wanted her to tell me about the first experience in her life that might relate to why she always felt she didn't fit in. She described an incident that had occurred when she was an infant. She didn't know how old she was but knew that she didn't yet know how to talk, but she could hear. She was in a baby crib, and she could hear her mother and her grandmother arguing in the kitchen, the next room. The grandmother said, "I told you that you should not have had that baby. The baby's father wouldn't marry you. There is no place for her in this world." At that point, the girl again cried profusely. That was the insight part of the technique.

Next, I wanted to reprogram her thinking about those experiences. I said, "You know, it doesn't sound to me like you had a very nice grandmother. I know I sure don't like her from what you described. To say the least, she didn't seem to have the sensitivity or ability to love and accept you and to cherish you the way you deserved, the way most grandmothers would have done. But what if you'd had the most wonderful grandmother in the whole world, one with the Christlike qualities of love, compassion, and empathy? [I don't do religious counseling, but I knew she was a Christian, so I used that reference.] What if you'd had that kind of grandmother? What would she have said?"

Her tears turned to a big smile, and she said, "She would have said, 'What a beautiful baby! I'm so glad we have her!'"

I said, "And that is what most grandmothers would have said. Unfortunately, you were stuck with a mean-spirited grandmother who was incapable of giving you or unwilling to give you the love you deserve. But that's not your fault."

Then I said, "Now let's go back to when you were three years old and playing naked on the floor with your dolls. If you'd had the most wonderful mother in the world, one with all those wonderful qualities, what would she have said? Or better yet, if you were the mom, and it was your three-year-old daughter, what would you have said?"

She responded, "I would have said, 'Honey, it's not good hygiene to play on the floor without any panties, so you can get dressed and play, or you can get up in the bed and play.'"

I said, "You mean you wouldn't have told her she was a bad girl?"

She responded, "Of course not!"

"Well then, were you a bad girl?" I asked.

She responded, "Of course not."

Once again, the key idea was reinforced: it was not her fault. She left that day like a different person.

Now, uncovering work does not always bring results that are so dramatic or achieved so quickly, but this case shows that things that happened long ago can have an impact on your life in the present.

If you were to see me in my office and were interested in pursuing this technique, I would say the following:

> As you continue to relax in this manner, I am going to teach you a technique to understand and let go of whatever has been blocking you. If we can find an early origin of the problem that is blocking you from success, this will create what we call an "affect bridge." By finding the origin, it bridges the gap, so to speak.
>
> We are going to use a technique called hypnoprojection. I want you to imagine sitting in front of a giant screen, and in just a moment, as I count backward from five to one, imagine the film rewinding. When we get to one, a picture will come into focus on that screen. That picture will tell you about some past experience in your life related to the problems in the present that are blocking you from being your best self. We are using hypnoprojection because by imagining watching a movie of your past, you do not have to relive it, in case there was something traumatic. Rather, you imagine that it is a documentary, and you are the narrator of that documentary. It is a documentary about your life.

While uncovering, or regression, is one of many strategies, and a powerful one, I utilize to assist in learning to understand the origins of self-sabotaging or self-handicapping behavior, I must stress that because emotional material is often forthcoming, this technique should be done only by a hypnotherapist licensed in one of the mental health fields.

Reframing

A therapy approach from the cognitive behavioral therapy (CBT) theoretical model that seems especially important for athletes is called reframing. If you are a golfer, for example, I might get you to think about yips, or errors, not failures, and how both bad and good shots are experiences from which we can learn. A story I often tell about how reframing works is as follows.

Several years ago, an attorney came to see me. He said that the night before a big trial, he would feel so much anxiety that he would overprepare to the point that he did not get enough sleep, and he was thus not at his best when he got to court. I knew from our history-gathering session that he enjoyed sports and had played football in high school, so I asked him if he remembered the feelings he'd had the night before and morning of a big game. He acknowledged that he did.

I said, "I'm sure you probably felt some butterflies in your stomach, but I'll bet that as soon as the action started, they went away." He said I was correct, and I then asked, "So would you call those feelings, those butterflies, anxiety?"

He responded, "No, I don't know what I would call them but definitely not anxiety."

I said, "How about anticipation? Or excitement?"

He agreed those were better descriptions of what he'd felt before a big game.

I said, "And that is what you are feeling the night before a big trial. Anxiety is a form of fear. You are not afraid. Just the opposite: you are ready to get on with the action—ready to rumble, as the legendary boxing announcer Michael Buffer used to say before a fight, coining the statement."

Once that reframing had taken place and the client saw his feelings as excitement, anticipation, or readiness, his response to the situation changed drastically. He reported later that the night before his next trial after our session, he slept like a baby, and he woke up alert and refreshed and put on his A game.

Other Cognitive-Behavioral Approaches

CBT is a popular current psychotherapy approach. I often use CBT embedded into my hypnotic suggestions, including work on improving peak performance. One story about this approach is as follows.

I was teaching a night psychology class at the University of South Alabama. In those days, I had not yet learned hypnosis. I was discussing the famous psychologist Albert Ellis, who noted that most people believe a particular stimulus situation, which we'll call "A" leads to "B," which is the response or reaction. (In the class, I diagrammed it on the blackboard; with clients in my office, I use a sheet of paper.) But Ellis said that was not correct: the response is not B; rather, it is C. B is your "belief system," or what you tell yourself about A, which causes C.

I had two police officers in the class who were working on degrees in criminal justice. They often came to class in uniform and always sat next to one another. One of the officers said, "Doc, I know what you are saying, but I disagree. I am a law enforcement officer and have a very stressful job. My doctor tells me I now have a stomach ulcer because of stress. So it sounds like my job is A, and my response is B, the ulcer."

I asked him to describe his job, and he said, "Well, we ride in a patrol car, and people give us no respect. They call us words like *pig*. People are shooting at us, and I am having trouble sleeping at night."

It appeared his fellow officer was calm and cool, so on a hunch, I took a chance and called on him. I said, "The two of you are partners, right?" After he affirmed that and said they rode in the same patrol car, I said, "How about you describe your job to the class?"

He responded, "Well, he's right. People often don't respect us. And they do call us names. One time, somebody threw a brick at the car." His account was different from his partner's assertion that people were shooting at them. "But I don't lose any sleep over it. It's just a job."

I responded, "Wait a minute! You don't lose any sleep over it, and you view it as just a job. Let me guess: you don't have an ulcer."

He answered, "Of course not."

His partner with the ulcer said, "Screw you!" to his partner—at least I think it was to his partner and not to me.

So you see, what you tell yourself about a situation determines your reaction to that situation.

In this chapter, I have presented some of my general approaches to incorporating other therapy approaches into hypnosis. Those included are examples of the general concepts I use when working with athletes.

CHAPTER 7

Inspirational Stories and Affirmations

I find storytelling to be an effective teaching technique with all clients, especially athletes. When you hear a story about others, you often understand more clearly how the phenomenon might apply to you (and are less likely to be defensive) than if you are given direct suggestions. Dawn Daniels of Stone Soup Productions is credited with my favorite quote about storytelling: "I believe in the power of story to awaken, to challenge, to enrich, and to heal. Come sit by my fire."

Many famous sports stars have used self-hypnosis. In one case, a professional football field-goal kicker would go through a prekick ritual that involved a hypnotic approach and would then visualize the ball going through the uprights. Interestingly, field-goal kicking appears to be different from the rest of the game of football, perhaps because there is more time to think before kicking. For this reason, opponents often call a time-out before a kicker attempts a clutch field goal. This is called "icing the kicker."

Inspirational movies about sports are helpful with athletes more than with any other client group. I often suggest watching the Kevin Costner movie *For Love of the Game*. I especially want clients to see what the pitcher does to block out distractions, especially when playing in an opposing team's ballpark. The home crowd is typically hostile, heckling the pitcher and telling him what a bum he is and so on. In the movie, he deals with this by saying to himself, "Clear the mechanism," and it is as if he suddenly becomes deaf, blocking out all sounds. I believe this to be a form of self-hypnotic trance induction.

There are numerous inspirational movies focusing on football and other sports, and they generalize from one sport to another. For example, I once heard about a college basketball coach who had his team watch *Remember the Titans*, a movie that is about a high school football team but has an inspirational message that crosses all sports. At the end of this book, in appendix C, I've included a listing of other inspirational movies about sports, especially golf. In appendix A, there is a list of affirmations from a variety of sources. Some are identified, and others are anonymous. Pick the relevant ones; print them out in large, bold letters; and paste them on your walls, mirrors, or lockers—anywhere that will remind you to think of success.

I often remind athletes who are actively competing of the song Whitney Houston recorded as NBC's theme song for their production of the 1988 Summer Olympics in Seoul, South Korea, entitled "One Moment in Time," written by Albert Hammond and John Bettis. The lyrics are inspiring and reinforce the importance of seizing the moment, when it avails itself, to be the best you can be, excel, and do something great. If you are the type to download tunes, I encourage you to download it or perhaps just download the words, which are inspirational.

Yet another motivational event I sometimes refer to is a talk that the famous Hall of Fame defensive back Ronnie Lott gave to the New Orleans Saints football team the night before their 45–7 shellacking of the Oakland Raiders in a preseason game in August 2009. Drew Brees, who became the MVP of the Super Bowl after that season, said, "Coach ran off all of his accolades, which are unbelievable and impressive." He added, "But he told us that he'd trade it all to get one more chance to compete." Brees noted that competitors always have that feeling. He said Lott talked about their "window of opportunity" and the sacrifice they needed to make as players for themselves and the good of the team. Interestingly, that year, the Saints went to their first Super Bowl and won the world championship.

Another motivational tool I use that you might appreciate has to do with perseverance when the going gets tough. It is a poem called "Never Quit on the Uphill" by Dr. Carl Touchstone, a dentist who was an avid megamarathon runner. Carl was born in Gulfport, Mississippi, but lived many years in Laurel, Mississippi. He didn't start running until he was thirty-four, and he died of prostate cancer in 2000 at the age of fifty-nine. By his own account, he started running in 1974, when he weighed 256 pounds and had high blood pressure (160/100). He had watched his father and brother die from heart failure at the ages of fifty-three and thirty-three, respectively, so he started walking three miles a day for the first six months, and then he began to jog. After a while, he started entering 5Ks and then longer runs, such as 10Ks. In 1977, he ran his first marathon in a respectable time of 3:31 (the best I ever did was 4:20). This Mississippi boy became known nationally and internationally in the ultra circuit. In fact, there is an ultramarathon named after him in Desoto National Forest, just south of Laurel, Mississippi.

I saw Carl's poem published in the Gulf Coast Running Club's newsletter years ago. I was a member then, and I reprinted it. However, I lost that copy in Hurricane Katrina. I recently saw "Never Quit on the Uphill" reprinted online by an author who wrote a book about maximizing potential. While the poem refers to running, the concept applies to all sports and, for that matter, to life. For copyright reasons, I cannot reprint the whole poem here, but he talked about when the going gets tough and one is thinking about quitting, or tempted to at least stop and rest, persistence will be rewarded.

The poem begins,

> When things are hard and the going gets tough
> When the trail is steep and the footing is rough

Carl talks about the great temptation to quit when faced with difficulty, but the poem ends with the following:

> Then the crest of the hill comes into full view
> And we reach the top of this problem so new.
>
> Cruising downhill now with strength in our stride
> The wind in our face, with joy and with pride
> "Thank you God for your grace and good will
> To see that we didn't quit on the uphill."

CHAPTER 8

Recovering from Injury and Returning to Training and Competition

Over the years, I have worked with several golfers who recovered from injuries, whether overuse injuries, tendinitis, or shoulder pain, or from surgeries, especially knee replacements or hip replacements in older athletes, and wanted to return to playing. The following is an overview of dealing with those issues.

A good starting place for review in this area is the book *Comprehensive Sports Injury Management: From Examination to Return to Sport* (Taylor et al. 2003). The authors address the psychological implications of injury and the psychological issues encountered in rehabilitation. They devote an entire chapter to the psychological concerns of return to sport. The senior author, Jim Taylor, has been a consultant to the US and Japanese ski teams and is a former US top-twenty-ranked alpine ski racer who competed internationally. He is also a certified tennis-teaching professional, a second-degree black belt and certified karate instructor, a marathon runner, and an Ironman triathlete. He talks about the importance of athletes' trust in the sports medicine provider. Considerable time must be spent in dealing with these issues.

Taylor also wrote an earlier book (Taylor and Taylor 1997) in which the authors focus on emotional factors, such as fear and loss of confidence or motivation, which often can be harder to overcome than the physical injury itself.

If you have been injured, working with your medical providers regarding the real physical limitations is of particular importance, but working with a sports psychologist can be beneficial as well, especially if he or she uses sports hypnosis to deal with the emotional components of the injury and recovery.

There are numerous hypnotic scripts that are effective for pain reduction. My previous book on sports hypnosis includes a wide variety of resources on which I base my approaches to pain management, some of which I will share below, as well as related works having to do with the mind-body connection as it relates to physical pain and healing. This combined approach allows me to incorporate two goals: First, if you are working on improving performance but later develop an injury, the focus can easily change to teaching you how to lower subjective pain. Second, if the presenting problem is pain, once you have recovered and are ready to return to sport, the hypnotic experiences will transition well into using hypnosis to improve performance.

Just as with any client I consult for pain management, I believe it is important to let any athlete with pain know that seeing a psychologist does not indicate that anyone thinks the pain is all in his or her head. I tell athlete clients, "Of course, if you did not have a brain, the pain would have nowhere to register, so in a way, it is in your head! But no one doubts that you have a real injury that is causing the pain. After all, we have technology, such as x-rays and MRIs, to show us pictures of the affected area, but the psychological aspects of pain may account for why some athletes adapt to the injury and pain, whether it required surgery or not, and others take longer or perhaps never play again."

Some of my nonathlete pain patients also ask me if their pain management physician sent them to see a psychologist because he or she believes the pain is all in their head. In addition to the above discussion about the brain signaling pain, I sometimes say, "You said your pain today is [for example] a seven on a ten-point scale, correct? But what if you left here and got word that your best friend, your spouse, or another loved one tragically and unexpectedly had died? What do you think would happen to that pain number?"

Invariably, they respond, "It would probably go up to a ten."

"Okay, and what if you learned you had just won a two-hundred-million-dollar lottery? What would happen?"

Invariably, they say, "Well, it would go down. Maybe to zero."

The point is that we have what is called the mind-body connection, or the mind-body cycle. Pain affects your emotions, but emotions can also affect pain levels. I currently work part-time in a pain-management clinic and am referred to there as their pain psychologist, and my work with pain patients dovetails nicely with working with athletes who have overuse or other injuries with related pain. I was on the board of directors of the Southern Pain Society for four years, and before taking a leadership position with them, I was a member of that group for several years. Such organizations stress the importance of an interdisciplinary approach to pain, including orthopedic specialists, pain-management specialists (MDs, many of whom were originally trained in anesthesiology), surgeons, psychologists, and physical therapists, among others.

I tell clients two personal stories. The first involves my first American Society for Clinical Hypnosis workshop in Saint Louis in 1978. I was just learning to do hypnosis in an introductory workshop in 1978. One of the lecturers was teaching the entire group to do self-hypnosis. After the large lecture group, we broke down into small discussion groups. I told the instructor, "I was able in the large group to put myself into a trance state and imagine that the lower right quadrant of my back was a block of ice, numb and insensitive to pain. It worked in getting rid of the pain from a recent back injury. But as soon as I come out of trance, the pain returns. How do you give yourself a posthypnotic suggestion to stay pain free?"

Her answer had nothing to do with hypnosis or self-hypnosis. She responded, "Well, Joe, why do you need that pain?"

I realized that throughout the meetings, if I was interested in what a particular speaker was saying, I was unaware of the pain, but when I became bored, I felt the need to move to adjust my back, and the pain was there. In her small group, there was a guy I disliked because he tried to dominate the group discussion. Whenever he spoke, I thought, *Damn, my back is hurting!* When the instructor, whom I liked, spoke, however,

I felt no pain. The injury was there physically and showed up on x-rays, but how much I attended to it determined how much subjective pain I experienced.

The second story I tell about pain and the power of the mind involves my running career. After I became competitive in my age group in the 5K and 10K races put on by my local running club, I had a non-running-related back injury. I was cross-training with weights and was doing some arm exercises with relatively light dumbbells, and when I went to put one of them down, reaching forward in an awkward position, I felt a pull in my back. By the next day, the pain was pretty severe, so I went to see a chiropractor buddy who was an ultramarathoner (fifty miles or more) and whom I earlier had helped quit smoking with hypnosis, as smoking had interfered with his effective running. He did some x-rays, diagnosed the condition as a vertebra out of place, and did chiropractic adjustments. He then told me to rest for a few days without any vigorous exercise.

I said, "But I'm entered in a 5K race this Saturday," referring to a race two days away.

He asked, "Joe, could you just go out and run at a leisurely pace and not try to push yourself to compete?" I must have glared at him for a moment, because then he said, "No, I guess you can't do that, can you? So just take four ibuprofen before the race and go blow it out."

I followed his instructions, and I did well in the race and felt no pain.

Now, I know that my injury and my pain before that race likely were not as significant as what you may be dealing with right now, but I think it is a good example of the power of the mind to compete if the motivation is strong enough. I don't want you to go against your doctor's or trainer's orders; I just want to help you not to fear competing within the boundaries they create for you.

In addition to the psychological aspects that determine the rapidity of return to sport, if the above-mentioned adaptation does not occur as fast as the prognosis indicated it should, negative psychological symptoms, such as anxiety, depression, and anger, might develop. While relatively minor injuries might cause minor emotional symptoms, more serious injuries, because they are unexpected and seem uncontrollable, often result in unfamiliar feelings and questions about whether you will ever play again or at least play at as high a level.

I deal with lessening an athlete's pain in much the same way as lessening nonathletic pain. One technique I like is a metaphor I call the master control room. In fact, this is a takeoff on the technique I described in case number four in chapter 2, with the golfer who suffered anxiety. I am going to repeat the metaphor but change *anxiety* to *pain*. After you have put yourself in a deeply relaxed state using the technique I taught you earlier, concentrate on the following:

> I invite you to imagine something as I describe it to you. There used to be a ride called Body Wars in Walt Disney World Resort's Wonders of Life pavilion at Epcot. Body Wars was a motion-simulator attraction. On the ride, as I remember it, riders shrank and carried out a mission inside a human body. It was an educational ride in which you explored the heart, the lungs, and other internal organs. It was based upon the Advanced Technology Leisure Application Simulator (ATLAS).
>
> Imagine you could, in a similar manner, be in a shrunken state and be projected inside your own brain. I think of the brain as the control center for the body. I liken the human brain to the NASA space center in Houston. Now, I have never been to a NASA facility, but I have seen a lot of movies about astronauts, and the astronauts are always communicating with the NASA space center in Houston. For example, they say, "Come in, Houston." I say: "You are familiar with that, are you not?" (I have always gotten a nod to this question). I add: "The brain is, in fact, your control center.
>
> Imagine you come upon a lot of technical instruments in the brain: monitors, gauges, controls, and switches.

Imagine a monitor on the left that measures pain, and just to the right of it, there is one for relaxation. Regardless of what your feelings are right now, imagine relaxation being low—only a one on a ten-point scale—and pain being high—a nine on a ten-point scale. Imagine you begin to adjust the levels using knobs like rheostats.

As you turn the relaxation knob clockwise from a one to a two with your right hand, you simultaneously turn the pain knob counterclockwise from a nine down to an eight with your left hand. You notice a little difference, so you proceed, turning relaxation up to a three with the right hand and, with the left, turning pain counterclockwise down to a seven. You continue by turning the relaxation knob up to a four and the pain down to a six. Now you notice something curious and interesting: when you turn the relaxation up, the pain decreases automatically; the knob turns by itself. So with the next move, you decide to experiment ... You turn relaxation up to a five, but your left hand is not quite touching the pain knob; your fingers rest just outside the knob, yet sure enough, it turns by itself, down to a five.

This makes sense because pain and relaxation are incompatible responses—they are mutually exclusive. I learned a long time ago, back in my graduate school years, that we never unlearn a negative behavior; instead, we learn a positive behavior that is incompatible with the old negative one.

Now excited, you proceed with the process ... You turn the relaxation knob up to a six, and pain decreases to a four ... Then up to a seven and a three, and so on. You might go all the way up to a nine on relaxation and down to a one on pain. A perfect ten on relaxation is likely a sleep state, and we do not want to go down to a zero on pain, lest you go out and further injure the affected area. Remember, pain is your signal … It reminds you that something needs attention, like the signal on your dashboard that tells you when to check the engine. Without that signal, you might burn up the motor. So in a way, a slight amount of pain is a friend who warns you when something is wrong. Of course, if you are doing this work at bedtime, then a ten on relaxation and a zero on pain are fine.

Cellular-Healing Script

Another script I often use with clients with injuries and anticipated surgeries is one I reported in a published case study regarding successful blepharoplasty using only hypnosis and a local anesthetic (Tramontana 2008). It is useful for preparing you if you need surgery and for recovery after surgery or injury.

As an athlete, you have likely heard of muscle memory. This notion means that muscles have intelligence. In fact, every cell in your body has intelligence, and that intelligence is what allows your body to heal. Think about it: Have you ever broken a bone, or have you known someone who broke a bone? The patient usually goes to an emergency room or clinic. After x-rays have been taken and the bone has been reset, the limb is likely put in a cast or brace of some sort to immobilize that area. Then the patient might be prescribed pain medication and sent home for healing to begin. Patients are scheduled for periodic returns to the medical provider to check the progress and perhaps for placement in a smaller cast or brace, until they are discharged from medical care. Perhaps there is a referral to a physical therapist.

However, the doctor, cast technician, pain medication, follow-up visits, and physical therapist do not do the healing. The body heals itself step by step, cell by cell. The body knows what to do and how to do it. The experiences with doctors, casts, and others only set the stage for healing to occur, but ultimately, your body heals itself.

Now consider another example. Let's say you have a bad cut or laceration that needs stitches. You go to a hospital or urgent care clinic. A nurse cleans the wound. The doctor then stitches it up, the nurse puts on an ointment and a bandage, and the doctor perhaps prescribes an antibiotic to prevent infection and then sends you home for healing to begin.

Again, the doctor, nurse, stitches, ointment, bandage, and antibiotics do not do the healing. The body heals itself step by step, cell by cell. All the other people and procedures just set the stage for healing to begin. Remember, your body knows what to do and how to do it.

Lingering Injuries

Some golfers report lingering injuries. It has long been a puzzle why athletes with similar conditions heal differently or at different rates. For example, say two NFL running backs have the same knee injury according to diagnosis, the same surgeon, and the same prognosis for return to playing, but one returns to the game in the expected time or even sooner, and the other never plays again. People often theorize that the differences are mental.

Taylor et al. (2003) describe negative reactions of an athlete to an injury as normal to some degree, because the condition or state is unfamiliar, among other reasons. If the player does not go through the normal adaptation processes and the injury lingers longer than the objective data indicates it should, a clinical (perhaps mental) condition likely has arisen.

I had the good fortune of attending a presentation by Dr. Dabney Ewin, a former president of the American Society for Clinical Hypnosis, put on by the New Orleans Society for Clinical Hypnosis in 2008. The presentation was entitled "Ideomotor signaling in the Treatment of Psychosomatic Illness." I assumed that learning more about Dr. Ewin's approach would be of benefit to me in working with psychosomatic illness, especially since I work part-time at a pain-management clinic. I came to realize, however, that I could adapt his techniques to my work with athletes with lingering injuries as well.

Dr. Ewin teaches his patients ideomotor signals: raising the index finger signals "Yes," the middle finger signals "No," and the thumb signals "I'm not ready to deal with that" or "I don't want to answer yet." In his presentation and in his book with a similar title (Ewin, 2006) describes seven common causes of psychosomatic disorders: conflict, organ language, motivation, past experience, identification, self-punishment, and suggestion. His theory is that since the left brain controls verbal behavior, logical and analytical thinking, and so forth, when questioned while in a hypnotic state, the client might still try to analyze what is the most logical answer. The right brain, on the other hand, controls nonverbal behavior, creativity, reflexive or instinctive responding, and, in general, emotions and feelings. Therefore, his questioning always involves language such as "Do you feel [or do you sense] that you are being affected by conflict?" [or the other six common causes].

Kroger and Fezler (1976, 46) postulate that one cannot talk to the unconscious. Rather, they believe the ideomotor signaling technique acts like a projective technique and, as such, can elicit valuable information.

I had learned about ideomotor signaling many years before and used it at times but not in hypnotic uncovering of the origins of psychogenic disorders. One difference from Ewin's approach is that I always give the client an "I don't know" signal (the pinkie finger). I request that the client use that response only as a last resort; otherwise, it is too easy for the client to avoid a "Yes" or "No" signal. One observation I find amusing is that when instructed to answer with their fingers, some clients give a "Yes" signal while shaking the head from side to side (a negative response) or a "No" signal while nodding up and down (a positive response).

Specific techniques for use with athletes follow.

If you are having trouble recovering from injury and have not returned to golf or are performing below your standard for yourself, use self-hypnosis, and present the following:

> One of the things that causes symptoms is *CONFLICT.* A conflict occurs when a person wants to do one thing but feels he or she should do the opposite. You feel as if you are being pulled in two directions. Answer with your fingers. Do you feel or sense that you are taking longer to heal and return to competition than the doctors expected because of some conflict?

If the yes finger rises, ask yourself,

> Would it be all right for you to bring that conflict up to the surface?

If the yes finger goes up, then say,

> Okay, tell yourself what you feel this conflict might be about.

Whether the answer was "Yes" or "No," after reviewing conflict, go on as follows:

> *ORGAN LANGUAGE* is something else that can cause symptoms. Organ language refers to phrases in our everyday speech that include a negative mention of a body part, such as "I feel like I have been stabbed in the back," or "I feel like I am falling apart." Do you feel that organ language might be causing the symptoms?

If the yes finger rises, say,

> Would it be all right to think some more about it?

Continuing, if you still have no answers as to what might be blocking you from recovering, present the following:

> Another thing that might cause symptoms is *MOTIVATION*. A person can be motivated to have a symptom because it seems that symptom helps solve some other problem—for example, when a student gets sick before an examination or a soldier gets sick before an impending battle. I know how badly you want to return to practice and competition [some athletes, such as NFL players, might like missing summer camp or certain practices, but some coaches will not let athletes compete if they haven't practiced], but do you feel or sense that in some way, you have motivation to hold on to the pain?

This question can be telling. If your recovery to play golf is slower than expected, follow through with all these possible causes.

> Another possible cause of symptoms is *PAST EXPERIENCE*. This refers to an emotionally charged event that might cause immediate onset of symptoms or sensitize you so that some other analogous event will activate the symptom. Answer with your fingers: Do you sense or feel that your lingering injury problem started with a significant experience from your past?

If the yes finger rises, ask,

> Would you like to go back and make a subconscious review of everything that was significant to you in that episode?

If the yes finger rises, say,

> Did this incident occur before age twenty? If not before age twenty, let's move forward in five-year increments.

If before age twenty, we'll move backward in five-year increments.

Depending on the determination of when the incident occurred, ask,

> Is it all right to orient your mind to what happened before age ____ that relates to the present problem with difficulty in getting over this injury?

Next, continue with the following:

> Another possible cause of symptoms is *IDENTIFICATION*. Do you sense or feel that you are identifying with another person who had the same or a similar symptom?

If the yes finger rises, a line of questioning ensues. For example,

> Would it be okay to go back and review this issue? With whom are you identifying? Is this identification behavior rational and successful in helping you in some way? Would this person want you to identify with him or her in having this problem?

Continue with the following:

> Yet another possible cause of symptoms is *SELF-PUNISHMENT*. The word *pain* comes from the Latin root *poena*. This is also the root for the words *punishment*, *penitentiaries*, *penal colonies*, and so on. When we are young and get our hands caught in the cookie jar, we might be admonished, sent to our rooms, put in time-out, and so on. As adolescents or adults, if we do something wrong and feel guilt, we might punish ourselves with a symptom, such as pain.

> With punishment enforced by others, there is usually a time limit (for example, a jail sentence, a probationary period, or some other enforced punishment period). The problem with self-punishment is the lack of a cutoff. If you were to give yourself three lashes, the pain would be over after the third lash. So ask yourself: Haven't you already been punished and suffered enough? Ask yourself if you feel or sense that in some way, your difficulty in healing, feeling better, and returning to competition is a form of self-punishment. Use your finger signals.

Lastly, continue as follows:

> Yet another cause for continuing the symptom is the *POWER OF SUGGESTION*. This refers to a suggestion, perhaps given to you by someone else, maybe a person in authority, that is negatively impacting you and thus affecting your return to practice and competition.

If the yes finger rises, indicating a suggestion, say,

> Would it be all right to bring this up to a conscious level and discuss this suggestion? This can often be a factor that causes self-doubt and even self-sabotage. For example, has anyone in your past ever suggested that you would never be successful or would never amount to anything? Could this be the case? Because if this is the case, he or she obviously was wrong. Look at everything you have already accomplished. You have already proven the person wrong. Since that person is obviously fallible, wouldn't it be okay to delete that suggestion from your conscious mind?

In summary, ideomotor signaling can help you gain some insights about the psychodynamic causes of problems affecting your game and can help in gaining insights and formulating a treatment plan. Overall, I recommend a somewhat eclectic approach that includes hypnosis for uncovering (i.e., age regression) and hypnoanalysis via ideomotor signaling, cognitive-behavioral techniques, reframing, guided imagery, and any other techniques in the therapist's repertoire that will enhance return to sport after an injury. All of this is geared toward self-exploration regarding any blocks to full recovery and an improved golf game.

CHAPTER 9

Anxiety Disorders

Sometimes your golf game can be affected by performance anxiety or by issues other than the game itself. I begin this discussion with a classic inspirational poem by Walter D. Wintle, a poet of the late nineteenth and early twentieth centuries (not to be confused with Walter Winchell, the American newspaper and radio gossip commentator). The title is "Thinking" or "The Man Who Thinks He Can," depending on which revision you read. The original title was "Thinking," but in later reprints, it was changed to "The Man Who Thinks He Can."

> If you think …
> If you think you are beaten, you are;
> If you think you dare not, you don't.
> If you'd like to win, but think you can't,
> It's almost a cinch you won't.
> If you think you'll lose, you're lost,
> For out in the world we find
> Success begins with a fellow's will; It's all in the state of mind.
> If you think you're outclassed, you are;
> You've got to think high to rise.
> You've got to be sure of yourself before
> You can ever win a prize.
> Life's battles don't always go
> To the stronger or faster man;

> But sooner or later the man who wins
> Is the one who thinks he can.

In chapter 2, I discussed a technique I used with the golfer presented as case number four. I used the master control room metaphor to help him gradually reduce anxiety while increasing relaxation. The message is that relaxation and anxiety are incompatible responses; one precludes the other. As I noted earlier, the focus is on increasing the positive, and the negative will take care of itself.

Another technique I often use for decreasing anxiety, stress, and tension (I use the terms interchangeably) is the invisible barrier metaphor, which I have adapted from Havens and Walters (1989).

The invisible barrier metaphor is as follows:

> I do not know if you have any experience with horse farms, but if so, you know about the electric fences used to keep horses in their corrals. There are tiny strands of wire through which runs an electric current. Not the kind that would cause serious harm, just a sudden, sharp zap, like the kind you might get from switching on a light switch while standing on a carpeted floor.
>
> Horses, being pretty smart animals, learn quickly not to brush up against the fences. They learn so well, in fact, that the farmer or rancher can disconnect the electrical power or even remove the wires and replace them with string, and the horses still avoid going through. They are fenced in by nothing at all, by a thought or a memory, an invisible barrier that keeps them from venturing out.
>
> But if one horse accidentally goes through the invisible barrier, the other horses quickly follow through. Once they're out in the pasture, you would likely see them frolicking, running, and maybe even kicking up their heels. We don't know how they know where to go, but

we know that later in the day, when they get hungry, they find their way home to the barn as swiftly as they can. Because they want to be fed and warm, even if there is a fence in the way, it can be leaped over to reach their goal.

In the same way, consider if some of your blocks to peak performance are the result of some invisible barrier, perhaps a memory or doubt from the past, and realize that it has nothing to do with today's reality. Put it behind, filed away as ancient history, and focus on the here and now.

An example of the invisible barrier and the importance of the "I think I can; I know I can" philosophy is demonstrated in the history of the mile run. For many years, the so-called experts believed humans were physically incapable of running a mile in under four minutes. Roger Bannister accomplished the feat in 1954 with a new world record of 3:59.4. The headline read, "Bannister Breaks Four-Minute Mile!" Prior to that, the record of 4:06.4, set in 1937, lasted until 1942, when a pair of Swedes, Gunder Hägg and Arne Andersson, kept lowering each other's records between 1942 and 1945, eventually getting it down to 4:01.3. Only forty-six days after Bannister's feat, however, his main rival, John Landry, lowered the record to 3:57.9. So the so-called experts were proven wrong. Once Bannister ran the mile in under four minutes, the time continued dropping.

The current record at the time of this writing is 3:43.13, held by Hicham El Guerrouj of Morocco, set in 1999 in Rome. The female record is still not below four minutes but is inching closer; Svetlana Masterkova of Russia holds the record at 4.12.56, set in 1996. I find it interesting that these two records have not changed in the nine years since my 2011 sports hypnosis book.

This history is proof that mental blocks can affect all people, perhaps especially athletes.

CHAPTER 10

Substance Abuse and Other Addictive Behaviors in Athletes

*A bend in the road is not the end of the road
unless you fail to make the turn.*

—Anonymous

For those of you who do not have any negative habits involving substances, this chapter might not be relevant, although I'll bet you know someone to whom it applies. Many of you probably know golfers who have a drink or two during a round or perhaps several at the club after the day's golfing is over. They might even have one or two before they begin, supposedly to take the edge off.

I will tell you a story about this phenomenon in competitive sailing. My wife at the time, now ex-wife, is an avid sailor. Among sailors, there is a lot of drinking in the yacht club after a regatta, or after each day of a regatta if it covers multiple days. It seems some sailors especially like rum—maybe an old pirate-day thing.

One Friday evening prior to a two-day regatta that began the next morning, my ex's team members were having a number of cocktails at the yacht club. When I joined them, she proclaimed to me and the group, "Joseph just wrote a book on sports hypnosis. Why can't you hypnotize our team to do better tomorrow?"

I replied, "I don't hypnotize athletes who get wasted the night before the competition and drink a prerace beer the morning of the race." While

I was joking with her and her teammates—who, by the way, were excellent sailors and often won or at least placed in the regattas—I believe it to be a true statement or philosophy. If the outcome of a competition is important to you, be of sound mind and body before you begin.

I indicated in chapter 8 that some experience in pain management or at least knowledge of referral resources is helpful in working with athletes who are injured, and I believe that some knowledge of and experience in treating addictions is helpful in working with athletes who develop maladaptive patterns, such as drug and alcohol use and abuse. My book involving hypnotically enhanced treatment of addictions (Tramontana 2009) also fits well into this area. Psychologists using sports hypnosis need not be experts in addictions. They should, however, have a firm base in how to treat or make appropriate referrals for these conditions. If this is an issue for you, I invite you to seek services from a professional trained in this area.

I was invited in 1983 to be a special guest on the Wayne Mack radio show. Wayne Mack was a highly regarded longtime talk radio host on a New Orleans station. The topic for that particular show was cocaine abuse in professional sports. I admit that in those days, I was not well versed in this subject matter, although I had considerable experience in working with nonathlete drug abuse, so after doing some literature research, I agreed to do the show. At the time, I could not find much literature on the topic. There was a helpful book published a few years later titled *Drugs and the Athlete* (Wadler and Hainline 1989), with references mostly from 1983 and later.

The famous sportscaster, Jim Gray, who has broadcast sports all over the world including numerous Olympics, Super Bowls, World Series, NBA Finals, NCAA Final fours, Masters, all-star games, and boxing title fights, has an engaging new book titled *Talking to GOATS* (2020). While he has an interesting Chapter (Ch 9) regarding his interviews with Tiger Woods titled "TIGER: How a legend became Human," for our purposes here Chapter 8 is relevant. This Chapter is titled "Steroids: From Ben to Marion, the Breaking of Bonds."

The author notes that the "Steroid Era" almost certainly started long before we knew it. He said it likely began when the first soon-to-be doped athlete or soon-to-push-doping coach or adviser looked around at his or her sport, considered the rules of play, and decided to attempt to find a way around them. He noted that testers of drug cheats have always been, and will always be, playing catch-up. He said some argue that everybody seeks an edge, and even when the various leagues did develop testing, they almost always fell behind the science deployed by cheaters.

He said: "Look at the East Germans, the Soviet Union, and China. Doping has been going on forever, unabated, to the point where Olympians from Russia were banned from the Winter Games in 2018 (although some competed under the Olympic Athletes from Russia banner)."

This all reminds me of my drag-racing days in the '60s. We were always looking for an edge, a hidden enhancement to allow us to transpire the quarter mile faster. Often times, these minor "cheats" became incorporated as standard equipment on future new cars whose carmakers were advertising, for example, "getting from 0-60 faster."

While the most common issue discussed by the sports media at present is use of performance-enhancing drugs (usually anabolic steroids), some professional athletes are being suspended for taking substances they claim they did not know were on the forbidden list. It seems unclear if this is a true addiction or simply an obsession with getting better, stronger, faster, and so forth. Perhaps there is some degree of ignorance of or disregard for the consequences of getting caught. Some famous athletes appear to be neither ignorant of nor uncaring about sanctions and penalties, but they get caught anyway. These have included track star Marion Jones and cyclist Lance Armstrong. Famous baseball stars, such as Mark McGuire, who allegedly set the home run record while using performance-enhancement drugs; Barry Bonds; Alex "A-Rod" Rodriguez; and Manny Rodriguez, have been in the spotlight as well. There are cases of football players, especially professional offensive linemen, who allegedly use steroids to bulk up and increase strength.

Recently, the great Olympic swimming star of the 2008 Summer Olympics, Michael Phelps, made the news after being caught on film smoking marijuana. He was suspended from competition for a while. In one day in May 2009, the local sports page had three references to athletes who were in trouble because of drugs or alcohol. These stories included a NASCAR driver, Jeremy Mayfield, who was suspended for testing positive for an unnamed drug. NASCAR, as of that date, had not revealed the drug, stating only that it was not alcohol. The article said, "It is relevant to know what dangers the 42 other drivers were exposed to with Mayfield on the track." Other stories from that same day involved a brief note about Donté Stallworth, wide receiver for the Cleveland Browns and formerly a high draft choice of the New Orleans Saints. He was free on bail on a DUI manslaughter charge from March 14, 2009, when he struck and killed a man while driving his Bentley drunk. Another story from that same day was about NFL receiver Reggie Williams, who pleaded guilty and was sentenced to two years of probation for cocaine possession in a case in which a Taser was used to subdue him. The Stallworth situation appeared the most severe, as he was initially said to be facing a fifteen-year prison sentence if convicted. As it turned out, he pleaded guilty to DUI manslaughter and received a thirty-day sentence, two years of house arrest, and eight years of probation, as well as a lifetime suspension of his driver's license. He was able, however, to resume his football career.

Over the years, athletes have used various types of speed (amphetamines) to stimulate performance. Recent studies have shown, in fact, that coffee (caffeine) is helpful in moderate amounts, and it is not illegal or banned. Painkillers have been known to cause addiction in some famous players. For example, former All-Pro Super Bowl–winning quarterback Brett Favre admitted he'd become addicted to painkillers that allowed him to play each week (King 1996). He went through a rehabilitation program, and that facility now has a new gym, which I was told he paid for as a donation to the program after his rehabilitation there.

Then there are the illicit and even killer drugs. Len Bias, a drafted basketball player who was expected to be a fantastic pro, died from a cocaine overdose in 1986 before ever playing a professional game. In the first chapter of their book *Drugs and the Athlete*, Wadler and Hainline list many athletes who are now deceased because of drug overdoses and many more whose careers were shortened because of drug use and abuse. They note that the cocaine-related deaths of Bias and Don Rogers, a football player with the Cleveland Browns, were, in 1986, a major impetus to drug testing in sports. Surveys from that time frame suggest that cocaine was the number-one drug abused. Unlike amphetamines, however, cocaine was used more for social reasons than for performance enhancement.

Karch (2009) talked about the ergogenic effects of caffeine. He reported studies that show it improves performance and endurance during prolonged, exhaustive exercise, such as cycling or prolonged running. He noted that sports governing bodies, such as the IOC, ban excessive use of caffeine; however, even without exceeding the requirement of a testing limit of twelve milligrams per milliliter, improvement has been demonstrated with marathon runners. In short-term competition, with intense aerobic exercise of greater than 90 percent VO_2 max, improved time to exhaustion has been repeatedly confirmed, although the performance increment has not been great.

Karch also noted that in the 1990s, a great deal was written about the dangers of combining caffeine with ephedra or ephedrine in athletic supplements and about the increased risk of such combinations for producing cardiovascular disease. A great concern at present is the use of anabolic steroids. Because they improve strength and performance, they are attractive to many athletes. Scientific explorations into the mechanism of this effect and possible medical complications are limited because abusers routinely take doses that far exceed what any doctor could ethically administer.

In the early 1990s, competitive athletes stopped using nandrolone because it remained in the body for weeks and was therefore very responsive to testing, although it was considered effective. Precursors of nandrolone, such as 19-norandrostenenedione and 19-norandrostenediol, which were sold legally in health-food stores, soon became substitutes for nandrolone. However, they are rapidly converted to nandrolone and still lead to dire consequences if an athlete tests positive (Karch 2009, 611–612).

Eating Disorders

Jockeys and gymnasts are infamous for having eating disorders. To maintain a low enough weight level, they might use all sorts of techniques to maintain their weight, including purging. Ballet dancers often experience eating disorders as well.

Thompson and Sherman's 1993 book *Helping Athletes with Eating Disorders: A User's Guide* focuses on eating disorders in athletes. They report that before their publication, there was a dearth of literature in this area. They conclude in the epilogue, "We are reminded that people often think athletes are healthier than the general population. It is ironic, then, that the same characteristics that contribute to their prowess, along with aspects of their training and exercise, may also contribute to the development of eating disorders in too many athletes." They suggest that getting in shape is too often associated with restrictive dieting, and we need to somehow put real health back into the eating and exercise regimens of athletes.

Tobacco Addiction

While cigarette smoking is now uncommon in athletes, it still occurs. I worked at different times with two marathon runners who were smokers. Common wisdom tells us that when runners begin endurance training, they often decide to quit smoking on their own, but these two separate cases were still smoking. While neither was an elite runner, one of them had run several marathons but had not yet quit smoking. The other was a new convert to marathon running.

After the first quit smoking, he went on to run many more marathons and even some ultramarathons (fifty-milers). At one point, he was approached by a reporter from the local newspaper. It was National Smoke-Out Day, and the journalist was writing a story about smoking cessation. She approached the man, a local chiropractor, and said she knew he was a marathon runner who used to smoke. She asked if he would be willing to help readers by letting them know how he quit. He responded, "You need to go interview Dr. Joe Tramontana—he is the one who taught me to quit through hypnosis." The newspaper writer did interview me and wrote a nice article. I got a lot more referrals from her article than I had from any paid advertisements.

In summary, using hypnotic techniques, I have treated individuals who wanted to improve sports performance but also had issues with drug use and addiction. Hypnotic treatment of the two issues may or may not have occurred in the same sessions.

Psychologists working with athletes for injury and pain or for improved sports performance might only later become aware the clients are using or abusing substances. The good news is that the transition to focus on that problem can be easy. Likewise, athletes first referred or self-referred for drug issues can later be transitioned into working on improving sports performance.

The quote at the beginning of this chapter regarding the bend in the road reminds me of a story I often tell my addict clients (Tramontana 2009) in general and athletes who are using drugs as well. An author who wrote a book about recovery from addiction talked about working with a group of addicts. He said one of the guys in his group never spoke, not even a word. One day the author was talking with the group about choices related to their decisions about using drugs. He told them, "It is just like driving a bus. When you get to an intersection and must stop, you can decide to turn right, turn left, go straight, or even do a U-turn and go back the way you came."

The quiet client finally broke his silence. It was as if a lightbulb went off in his head, and he said, "I finally understand my problem. All these years, I've had a junkie driving my bus."

While I tell this story with a goal of introducing some levity into sessions, when dealing with athletes, especially at the professional level, the cost of using can be in the millions, and of course, wasting a career and potential as well as money is not the least bit funny. Haven't you wondered how some athletes could possibly lose a career and perhaps millions of dollars by using banned substances?

CONCLUSION

The human mind is a powerful phenomenon. Interestingly, nobody knows exactly what it is. We know the brain is an organ, but what we call *mind* cannot be extracted after death, as an organ can. The mind is an abstract concept. We do know, however, that the mind is so powerful that people can think of themselves as successful or think of themselves as failures, and often, their behavior will follow suit, just as they might think of themselves as sick and get sick, versus thinking of themselves as well.

In the introduction, I said that if you want to achieve goals, you must create a positive mindset made of beliefs that support the truth you desire in your future. I mentioned in chapter 1 that I ask all golfers and other athletes (although many believe golf to be the most cerebral game) the following:

1. What percentage of success in golf is mental?
2. What percentage of your practice time do you spend on the mental aspects of your performance and competition?

Again, the answers to the first question are usually anywhere from 50 to 90 percent, and the answer to the section question is often, astoundingly, zero.

As I stated earlier, self-hypnosis training will not necessarily improve the mechanics of your performance; that is for your golf coach to help you fine-tune. However, the mental techniques in the preceding chapters can certainly help you get your head on straight, as I have heard many golfers state. How many times have you heard people say that a golfer had a great swing but had "head problems"?

All of the suggestions in this book are to help you get your head on straight rather than letting it get in your way.

APPENDIX A

Affirmations

Below, I provide a long list of affirmations, and I suggest you pick and choose what works for you. Some of the quotes are attributed to more than one person. For example, both Thomas Jefferson and Ben Franklin are credited with the quote "I'm a strong believer in luck, and I find the harder I work, the more of it I have," and several people are credited with the statement "Luck: When preparation meets opportunity." A quote I find somewhat amusing is from famous former NFL football coach Don Shula, who stated, "Sure, luck means a lot in football. Not having a good quarterback is bad luck!"

Many of the following affirmative quotes are attributed to specific individuals, while a number of them have unknown authors. If there is no name below the quote, either it is anonymous, or I lost the author's name. In addition, I've described some of the people whose quotes I've included. Some, such as JFK, Robert Kennedy, William Faulkner, Shakespeare, and Mark Twain, of course, need no introduction.

> Ability is what you are capable of doing. Motivation determines what you do. Attitude determines how well you do it.

—Lou Holtz, famous football coach and current TV sports announcer

Do just once what others say you can't do and you will never pay attention to their limitations again.

—James R. Cook, author of *The Start-Up Entrepreneur*

Don't be afraid of failing because of a mistake; be afraid of failing to learn from a mistake.

Don't bother just to be better than your contemporaries or predecessors. Try to be better than yourself.

—William Faulkner

Efforts and courage are not enough without purpose and direction.

—John F. Kennedy

An error doesn't become a mistake until you refuse to correct it.

—Orlando A. Batista, Canadian American chemist and author

Excellence is the result of caring more than others think is wise, risking more than others think is safe, dreaming more than others think is practical and expecting more than others think is possible.

Great minds have purposes. Little minds have wishes.

—Washington Irving, an eighteenth- and nineteenth-century writer and diplomatbest known for his short stories "Rip Van Winkle" and "The Legend of Sleepy Hollow"

The greatest mistake you can make in life is to be continually feeling you will make one.

—Elbert Hubbard, an American writer and philosopher who
died with his wife aboard the RMS *Lusitania* when it was sunk
by a German submarine off the coast of Ireland in 1915

The greatest pleasure in life is doing what people say you cannot do.

—Walter Bagehot, a British journalist from the 1800s

He who is outside his door has the hardest
part of his journey behind him.

—Dutch proverb

I am not competitive. I simply win.

—Coloradojules

I honestly think it better to be a failure at something you
love than to be a success at something you hate.

—George Burns, one of my favorite comedians

If we all did the things we are capable of, we would astound ourselves.

—Thomas Edison

If you can't do extraordinary things, do
ordinary things extraordinarily well.

If you can't win, make the fellow ahead of you break the record.

It had long since come to my attention that people of
accomplishment rarely sat back and let things happen
to them. They went out and happened to things.

—Elinor Smith, pioneering female American aviator who was the
first woman test pilot and youngest pilot in the world at age sixteen

It is better to begin in the evening than not at all.

—English proverb

It is not because things are difficult that we do not dare;
it is because we do not dare that things are difficult.

—Seneca, a Roman philosopher

It's not who you are that holds you back; it's who you think you're not.

Keep away from people who try to belittle your ambitions.
Small people always do that, but the really great ones
make you feel that you, too, can become great.

—Mark Twain

Life is 10 percent what happens to you and
90 percent how you respond to it.

No one can predict to what heights you can soar. Even
you will not know until you spread your wings.

Nothing great was ever achieved without enthusiasm.

—Henry David Thoreau, nineteenth-century poet and philosopher

Obstacles are those frightful things you see
when you take your eyes off your goal.

—Henry Ford, founded Ford Motor Company and sponsored the development of the assembly-line technique of mass production

One important key to success is self-confidence. An
important key to self-confidence is preparation.

—Arthur Ashe, an American professional tennis player who won three Grand Slam titles and was the first black player selected to the US Davis Cup team and the only black man ever to win the singles title at Wimbledon, the US Open, and the Australian Open

Only those who dare to fail greatly can ever achieve greatly.

—Robert F. Kennedy

Opportunity dances with those who are already on the dance floor.

—H. Jackson Brown, American author best known for his inspirational, best-selling book *Life's Little Instruction Book*

Our doubts are traitors and make us lose the good
we oft might win by fearing to attempt.

—William Shakespeare

Practice makes perfect, so be careful what you practice.

—Author unknown, but this is one of my favorite quotes in working with athletes and nonathletes who've developed bad habits and keep repeating them

Progress is not created by contented people.

—Frank Tyger, nicknamed Mr. Times for his work as an editorial writer and cartoonist, among other things, with the *Trenton Times*

Put your heart, mind, intellect and soul even to your smallest acts. This is the secret of success.

—Swami Sivananda, a Hindu spiritual teacher, proponent of yoga and Vedanta, and founder of the Divine Life Society who was a physician in British Malaya before taking up monasticism

A smooth sea never made a skillful sailor.

—Author unknown, but I like this quote based on my experiences in learning to sail and sometimes praying for wind

Success is a lousy teacher. It seduces smart people into thinking they can't lose.

—Bill Gates

Success is that old ABC—ability, breaks, and courage.

—Charles Luckman, nicknamed the Boy Wonder of American Business when he was named president of the Pepsodent Toothpaste Company in 1939 at the age of thirty

Take calculated risks. That is quite different from being rash.

—General George S. Patton Jr.

There are no mistakes, only lessons.

—Unknown

There are no secrets to success. It is the result of preparation, hard work, and learning from failure. The person who really wants to do something finds a way; the others find an excuse.

—Colin Powell, retired four-star general who became George W. Bush's secretary of state and before that was twelfth chairman of the Joint Chiefs of Staff

Trouble is merely opportunity dressed in work clothes.

Victory is sweetest when you've known defeat.

The vision must be followed by the venture. It is not enough to stare up the steps—we must step up the stairs.

—Vance Havner, one of America's most traveled evangelists and author of many devotional books

We are what we repeatedly do. Excellence, then, is not an act, but a habit.

—Aristotle

Whatever you do, or dream you can, begin it. Boldness has genius and power and magic in it.

—Goethe (1749–1832), German author of *Faust* and other notable works, as well as a philosopher and diplomat

When I stand before God at the end of my life, I would hope that I would not have a single bit of talent left, and could say, "I used everything you gave me."

—Erma Bombeck, an American humorist who achieved great popularity for her newspaper column that described suburban life from the mid-1960s until the late '90s—this is another of my favorite quotes for athletes and anyone else seeking to achieve peak performance

Whether you think you can or think you can't, you're right.

—Henry Ford

You can do whatever you have to do, and sometimes you can do it even better than you think you can.

You can't win if you don't begin.

You must have long-range goals to keep you from being frustrated by short-range failures.

—Charles C. Noble, an American major general and engineer who worked on the Manhattan Project, led construction in Nuremberg after World War II, developed the early American ICBM program, and made the controversial yet successful decision to open Morganza Spillway in northern Louisiana for the first time to relieve pressure upstream and save New Orleans during the 1973 Mississippi Flood

You shouldn't compare yourself to the best others can do.

You miss 100 percent of the shots you don't take.

—Wayne Gretzky, NHL Hall of Famer

You're never as good as everyone tells you when you win and you're never as bad as they say when you lose.

—Lou Holtz

Thinking (The Man Who Thinks He Can)
If you think …
If you think you are beaten, you are.
If you think you dare not, you don't.
If you'd like to win, but think you can't,
It's almost a cinch you won't.

If you think you'll lose, you're lost,
For out in the world we find
Success begins with a fellow's will; It's all in the state of mind.

If you think you're outclassed, you are;
You've got to think high to rise.
You've got to be sure of yourself before
You can ever win a prize.

Life's battles don't always go
To the stronger or faster man;
But sooner or later the man who wins
Is the one who thinks he can.

—Walter D. Wintle

APPENDIX B

Recommended Reading

In addition to the techniques I have taught you regarding utilization of self-hypnotic techniques for improving your focus and concentration and, thus, your scores, familiarity with the writings of other experts in the field will give you a much broader understanding of the importance of mental training. Whether through suggestions from sports psychologists who do not use formal hypnotic techniques (but call their techniques mental training) or from hypnosis practitioners, the more exposure you have to this intelligence, the better you will play. This concept is especially important because negative habits and negative self-talk lead to almost certain self-sabotage.

Golf Books

There are a number of popular books about golf. Some give somewhat of a history of great players and great matches, and others focus on the technical aspects of the sport, such as those by Dr. Bob Rotella. A sampling of these are listed below. Some are just a fun, nostalgic read, and others are about improving your game.

> Frost, M. *The Greatest Game Ever Played: Harry Vardon, Francis Ouimet, and the Birth of Modern Golf.* New York: Little, Brown Book Group, 2003.

This book was a *Sports Illustrated* Best Seller Award winner. Two golfers from different worlds and different generations evolved into a legendary battle at Brookline in the 1913 US Open. Vardon, from Britain, was considered the greatest champion in the game's long history, and Ouimet, from Massachusetts, was three years removed from his youthful career as a caddie and had worshipped Vardon.

> Frost, M. *The Match: The Day the Game of Golf Changed Forever.* New York: Little, Brown Book Group, 2007.

In 1956, a casual bet between two millionaires pitted two of the greatest golfers of the era, Byron Nelson and Ben Hogan, against top amateurs Harvie Ward and Ken Venturi. The two professionals had fourteen major championships between them. The rest is history.

> Frost, M. *The Grand Slam: Bobby Jones, America, and the Story of Golf.* New York: Little, Brown Book Group, 2004.

In the wake of the 1929 stock market crash, an amateur golfer began a decade of unparalleled success. In four months, he won the British Amateur Championship, the British Open, the United States Open, and the United States Amateur Championship, an achievement so extraordinary that writers dubbed it the "Grand Slam."

> Gallwey, W. T. *The Inner Game of Golf.* New York: Random House, 1991.

Prior to the above book, Gallwey wrote three books on tennis and skiing, and his inner-game concepts have been accepted in many sports as well as in other areas of life. The above book was the first I read prior to working with my first professional golfer client in the 1980s. The general thesis is that one's mind, emotions, and confidence play a much larger role in golf than in almost any other sport. Gallwey notes that in tennis, the player is hitting and moving the ball over and over again while on the run, and in skiing, the skier is hurtling down a mountain, so those athletes' reactions are much more instinctual than intellectual. He adds that in eighteen holes of golf, the player actually hits the ball for no more than three or four minutes during a four-hour round, and the time between shots is the bane of the average player. Whether a player is brooding over having flubbed his last drive, dreading his next shot from a sand trap, or trying to line up a tricky six-foot putt, he is constantly grappling with self-doubt, fear of failure, tension, and even anxiety.

William Hallberg wrote three interesting books about golf:

Hallberg, W. *Perfect Lies: A Century of Great Golf Stories.* New York: Doubleday, 1990.

This book is an anthology of twenty-three classic short stories about golf. The stories are by such famous authors as F. Scott Fitzgerald (*The Great Gatsby*; *Tender Is the Night*; *The Curious Case of Benjamin Button*), John Updike (*The Witches of Eastwick*; *Rabbit, Run*), and a number of other writers. In the introduction, he says, "After all, golf is a very personal game in which each player is hostage to his own incompetence."

Hallberg, W. *The Soul of Golf.* New York: Doubleday, 1997.

This interesting book was described on the back cover as "witty and wise," a book that "will make you laugh out loud, swallow hard in the face of painful truths, and, ultimately, head yet again for your favorite golf course where fate lies in ambush."

Hallberg, W. *The Rub of the Green.* New York: Doubleday, 1998.

This work is a funny, touching, and moving novel that tells the story of one man's glorious victories and bitter defeats in the most challenging sport of life.

Hogan, B. *Power Golf.* New York: Gallery Books, 1948.

Ben Hogan was, of course, one of the true legends of golf. He died in 1997. He won the Masters Tournament in 1951 and again in 1953, and he was entered into the World Golf Hall of Fame in 1974. In this book, he is quoted as saying, "There is no such individual as a born golfer. Some have more natural ability than others, but they're all made." The book goes through the arduous steps he took to make himself a champion.

In the introduction, there is a reference to the great Bobby Jones (1902–1971), who won seven men's major championships. He is quoted, when talking about a normal golfer's desire to play the game well, as follows: "If golf is worth playing at all, it's worth playing right."

> Mack, G., and D. Casstevens. *Mind Gym: An Athlete's Guide to Inner Excellence*. Chicago: Contemporary Books, 2001.

This book was recommended by Coach Girouard, whom I mention in the acknowledgments. While she is a women's softball coach, she said this is the single book she recommends most to athletes.

Gary Mack, the first author, is a noted sports psychologist who has worked with professional athletes in most major sports. He explains how your mind influences your athletic performance as much as your physical skill does, if not more so. The book includes forty lessons and inspirational anecdotes from prominent athletes, many of whom he has worked with to build what he calls "mental muscle."

The foreword was written by baseball great Alex Rodriguez. One of the prepublication reviews was done by former vice president Dan Quayle, who is described as a four-handicapper. He says, "As an avid golfer, I recommend this book to anyone desiring to raise their productivity or to lower their handicap."

Jason Kidd, NBA All-Star and Olympic gold medalist with the US basketball team, said, "I read *Mind Gym* on my way to the Sydney Olympics and really got a lot out of it. Gary has important lessons to teach and you'll find the exercises fun and beneficial."

> Marx, J. *The Long Snapper: A Second Chance, a Super Bowl, a Lesson for Life*. New York: Harper, 2009.

Jeffrey Marx, author of the best-seller *Season of Life*, does a great job of describing the mental anguish experienced by Brian Kinchen, whom I mention in the acknowledgments, who was interviewed for my previous sports hypnosis book. The New England Patriots called Brian out of retirement to be the long snapper in the 2003 Super Bowl. Frank Deford, a *Sports Illustrated* writer, gave the book the following endorsement: "Don't we all long for one last chance? Don't we all dream to do it over again? Anybody who has ever had those pangs will love Jeffrey Marx's beautiful and uplifting story about a guy who had opportunity dropped into his lap. Do yourself a favor and read *The Long Snapper*."

As I noted in the acknowledgments, I had no idea when I interviewed Brian how much of the time he would spend talking about golf. I didn't know he played the game competitively. He told me that the year of Super Bowl 2003, he played in a tournament in April. He was winning the tournament, but when it came to the last hole, he felt a great deal of pressure and felt really nervous. He said he then told himself, "I just snapped the ball for the winning field goal in front of millions of people on the biggest stage there is in football. This putt is nothing compared to that!"

I said, "That's great. You reframed it to reinforce your own self-confidence and take the pressure off. So how did you do?"

He said, "I just drained it—knocked it in the back of the hole. I won the tournament and a nice prize check."

Murphy, M. *Golf in the Kingdom*. New York: Penguin, 1972, 1997.

As described earlier, this book was proclaimed by Viking Press as "a masterpiece on the mysticism of golf," according to the *San Francisco Chronicle*. As I noted in the above narrative, to fully appreciate this book, one would have to be interested in the metaphysical or a study of the extraordinary or metanormal experiences.

Rotella, R. *Golf Is Not a Game of Perfect*. New York: Simon and Schuster, 1995.

This is a book written for players. It is filled with delightful and insightful stories about golf and golfers with whom Dr. Rotella has worked. He was director of sports psychology for twenty years at the University of Virginia and has consulted with many of the world's leading golfers as well as some of the top golf organizations, including the PGA, LPGA, and Senior LPGA.

> Rotella, R. *Golf Is a Game of Confidence.* New York: Simon and Schuster, 1996.

This book is filled with anecdotes and inspirational instruction. It focuses on the most important skill a golfer can have: the ability to think confidently. Dr. Rotella helps readers revolutionize their own mental game and approach to course management, and he relates stories of the game's legendary figures. In other words, he allows the reader not only to get inside the ropes but also to get inside the heads of the game's greatest players in their most important moments.

Rotella, R. *The Golfer's Mind.* New York: Simon and Schuster, 2004.

The introduction notes that this book was actually first suggested to Dr. Rotella by Davis Love Jr., Davis Love III's dad, who encouraged him to write an instructional book on golf's mental challenges, organized by topic. He thought golfers should keep the book nearby at all times so that when they needed a refresher on a certain issue, they could consult the book, read it for a few minutes, and take away guidance regarding their difficulties. He gives his ten commandments of achieving peak performance, which range from (1) "Play to play great. Don't play not to play poorly" to (10) "Love your wedge and your putter."

Three other books by Dr. Rotella, all with interesting additions to the above listed ones, include the following:

> Rotella, R. *Your Fifteenth Club: The Inner Secret to Great Golf.* New York: Simon and Schuster, 2008.

Rotella, R. *The Unstoppable Golfer.* New York: Simon and Schuster, 2012.

Rotella, R. *How Champions Think.* New York: Simon and Schuster, 2015.

Saunders, T. *Golf: Lower Your Score with Mind Training.* Carmarthen, UK: Crown House, 2005.

Tom Saunders, MD, focuses on overcoming bad habits and swings by training your mind. His approach involves focusing completely on the shot you are about to take, developing positive thoughts and behavioral patterns, using mental imagery to improve your game, and achieving active relaxation. The book is also accompanied by a CD of exercises focused on creating peak performance in golf and other sports.

Books on Recovery from Injury

Taylor, J., K. R. Stone, M. J. Mullen, T. Ellenbecker, and A. Walgenbach. *Comprehensive Sports Injury Management: From Examination of Injury to Return to Sport.* Austin, TX: Pro-Ed, 2003.

Jim Taylor, PhD, is internationally recognized for his work in sports psychology and injury rehabilitation. He has been a consultant to the United States and Japanese ski teams, the US triathlon team, and the United States Tennis Association, and he has worked with injured athletes in a number of professional sports as well as athletes at lower levels. Kevin Stone, MD, is an orthopedic surgeon and chairman of the Stone Foundation for Sports Medicine and Arthritis Research. He specializes in sports medicine and is a physician for the US ski team as well as various ballet groups and is affiliated with the United States Olympic Training Center. Taylor and Stone, along with the other authors, take a comprehensive approach to dealing with injured athletes from diagnosis to return to the sport.

Taylor, J., and S. Taylor. *Psychological Approaches to Sports Injury Rehabilitation.* Gaithersburg, MD: Aspen Publications, 1997.

In this book, the authors note that injuries are inevitable for athletes. At some point, injuries might take athletes out of sports for extended times. They note that although most will recover physically, some athletes will suffer psychological effects that inhibit rehabilitation. For these competitors, regaining self-confidence and motivation and overcoming fear are often more difficult than their physical recovery.

Books on Substance Use and Abuse in Sports

Karch, S. *Pathology of Drug Abuse.* 4th ed. Boca Raton, FL: Taylor and Francis Group, 2009.

This book presents a comprehensive review of drugs of abuse and how they are and have been used by athletes attempting to improve their performance and endurance.

Tramontana, J. *Hypnotically Enhanced Treatment for Addictions: Alcohol Abuse, Drug Abuse, Gambling, Weight Control, and Smoking Cessation.* Wales, UK: Crown House, 2009.

This book includes scripts, strategies, techniques, and case examples to aid therapists in designing treatment plans for all addictions, whether working with an athlete or a nonathlete.

Wadler, G. I., and B. Hainline. *Drugs and the Athlete.* Philadelphia: F. A. Davis Company, 1989.

These authors give a rather comprehensive review of the state of drug abuse in sports up to that point in time. They give many case examples of athletes who blew their opportunities for greatness or had careers cut short because of drug use.

Gray, J. *Talking to GOATS*. New York: HarperCollins Books, 2020.

This book includes a foreword by Tom Brady. Brady said: This book is sports history about some of the greats by one of the greats, who was taking it all in on the sidelines, in the stands or the dugout, by the eighteenth green, courtside, or in the broadcast booth." Famous athletes discussed include Tiger Woods, but also Mike Tyson, Ali, Michael Jordan, Kobe, Lebron, and Phelps, among other "Stories You Never Heard."

APPENDIX C

Inspirational Sports Movies and Fun Golf Movies

There are several sports movies across a range of different sports that are inspirational and sometimes recommended by coaches, even ones in different sports, to get their competitors pumped up. Some even have theme songs that athletes listen to while training. A list follows.

Chariots of Fire

This 1981 British film tells the fact-based story of two athletes in the 1924 Olympics: Eric Liddell, a devout Scottish Christian who was running for the glory of God, and Harold Abrahams, an English Jew who ran to overcome prejudice. Liddell was not just a track athlete but also a union international rugby player and missionary.

Nominated for seven Academy Awards, the movie was a surprise winner of Best Picture. It beat out box-office hits *On Golden Pond* and *Raiders of the Lost Ark*. The movie won a total of four Oscars and was listed in the British Film Institute's list of Top 100 British Films. It was suggested that the title of the film is a reference to the line "Bring me my chariot of fire" from the William Blake poem adapted into the hymn "Jerusalem." This interpretation likely arose because that hymn is heard at the end of the film.

Liddell won gold in the 400-meter and bronze in the 200, while Abrahams won gold in the 100-meter. I read somewhere on the internet that the theme song of the great soundtrack was titled "Abraham's Hat."

Cinderella Man

This 2005 movie is a biography and drama that tells the story of James Braddock (Russell Crowe) during the Great Depression. He was a boxer who could no longer make a living by boxing after breaking his hand. He set out to do whatever it took to support his family. While working on the docks, with his preferred hand a little gimpy, he built up great strength in his nondominant arm, and when he got a chance to fill in as a last-minute substitute in a fight, he found that with that new weapon in his arsenal, he was even better than before the injury. In sum, James Braddock made possible what previously had appeared impossible.

For Love of the Game

This movie from 2000, based on the book of the same name, is about a supposedly over-the-hill baseball pitcher, played by Kevin Costner, who used a form of self-hypnosis. While the technique is not identified in the movie as self-hypnosis, when he is playing in another team's ballpark and fans are jeering him and trying to distract him, he uses a technique he calls "clear the mechanism." This temporary deafness is surely a hypnotic effect.

Hoosiers

This 1986 movie is a drama based on the true story of Coach Norman Dale (Gene Hackman), who took on a high school basketball team from a small town in Indiana. He faced a lot of challenges and obstacles while trying to lead his team to the state finals.

Miracle on Ice

This 1981 movie is the true story of the 1980 US Olympic hockey team and Herb Brooks, their coach (Kurt Russell). They faced many obstacles, and their opponent in the first game in the medal round was their Cold War rivals, the Soviets. The US team was the youngest in the tournament, composed exclusively of amateur players, and the youngest in US national team history. The US team beat the Soviets and went on to win gold by beating Finland in the finals.

The great sportscaster Al Michaels famously declared after the win, "Do you believe in miracles? Yes!" In 1999, *Sports Illustrated* named the miracle on ice the top sports moment of the twentieth century.

Prefontaine

This 1997 movie produced by Disney Productions is based on the life of distance runner Steve Prefontaine, known as Pre. He was an Olympic hopeful coached by Bill Bowerman in Oregon. Bowerman was the creator of the Nike running shoe, and in the movie, Prefontaine is a test subject for many of Bowerman's earlier shoes.

Prefontaine was considered for a long time to be the best long-distance runner in the history of American running.

Some of his quotes from the movie are quite inspirational, such as "Winning is not about who is the fastest but who can endure the most pain," and "I am going to work so that it's a pure guts race. In the end, if it is, I'm the only one that can win." One more that applies to all sports, other performances, and life is "To give anything less than your best is to sacrifice the gift."

Without Limits

This movie, released a year after *Prefontaine*, is also about Pre and Coach Bowerman. Billy Crudup plays Pre, and Donald Sutherland plays Bowerman. While the movie did not gross much at the box office, it received excellent reviews, and Sutherland won the Golden Globe for Best Supporting Actor.

Remember the Titans

This movie, filmed in 2001, was produced by Walt Disney Videos. I understand that many coaches in football and other sports have their players watch this inspirational movie about the will to win.

The Rocky Movies

Nearly everyone is familiar with Rocky Balboa (Sylvester Stallone), who, in *Rocky*, gets the chance of a lifetime as a replacement in a fight against the champion. As a no-name boxer, he gets to prove his potential and become who he was destined to be. There have been several sequels to *Rocky*, and the music has been extraordinary, including the tunes "Gonna Fly Now" from *Rocky* and "Eye of the Tiger" from *Rocky III*. Many athletes have used this music for years to keep them juiced, so to speak.

Golf Movies

The following are lists of movies gleaned from the internet that are said to be the best golf movies of all time. Three different rating lists follow. Some of the movies are inspirational, and some are just plain fun.

Golficity's list of the "10 Best Golf Movies of All Time" includes the following, in reverse order:

> 10. *A Gentleman's Game* (2001). A golf prodigy (Mason Gamble) learns valuable lessons while working as a caddie at an exclusive golf club. Gary Sinise plays the role of his mentor.
>
> 9. *Strokes of Genius* (2004). The full title is *Bobby Jones: Strokes of Genius*, which the next list has at number ten. It is a biographical drama based on the life of revered golfer Bobby Jones (Jim Caviezel). Rising quickly from amateur status to legend, he became renowned for his

intense persona and for winning an extraordinary number of tournaments.

8. *Dead Solid Perfect* (1998). A wild, down-and-out pro golfer (Randy Quaid) with a fed-up wife tries to get his life together before the US Open. He is desperate for his one shot at success. One review called the film "a golfer's paradise movie" and "a golf lover's film dream come true."

7. *Seven Days in Utopia* (2011). A young golfer (Lucas Black), after a blow-up with his father and coach, seemingly has scuttled his once-promising career. While driving on a back road in Texas, he crashes through the fence of an eccentric rancher played by Robert Duvall. The rancher makes an irresistible offer for the kid to spend a week with him in the tiny town of Utopia to see if he can change his life.

6. *Greatest Game Ever Played* (2005). This is a movie about a young blue-collar caddie (Shia LaBeouf) who fights class prejudice and fine-tunes his skills during off-hours at an exclusive country club. While his father disapproves, some admirers help him enter the 1913 US Open. The film is based on a true story.

5. *Caddyshack II* (1988). This is a fun, funny movie full of comedians, such as Chevy Chase, Dan Aykroyd, Jackie Mason, Dyan Cannon, Robert Stack, and Randy Quaid. This one is for fun more than inspiration.

4. *The Legend of Bagger Vance* (2000). Directed by Robert Redford, this movie follows a promising local golfer (Matt Damon) whose once-promising career and life were derailed by World War I. A Georgia socialite

(Charlize Theron), during the Great Depression, announces a high-stakes match featuring the greatest golfers of the era at her struggling family golf course. The local golfer is brought in to play alongside the stars, but his game is weak—until the enigmatic Bagger Vance (Will Smith) offers to coach him back into the great golfer he once was.

3. *Tin Cup* (1996). This movie is about a golf pro, Roy McAvoy (Kevin Costner), who has a bright future but whose rebellious nature and bad attitude cost him dearly. While working with his newest pupil (Rene Russo), a psychiatrist who happens to be the girlfriend of his PGA Tour star rival (Don Johnson), he falls for his student. After being humiliated by the star at a celebrity golf tournament, Roy decides to make a run for the PGA Tour as well as his love interest's heart.

2. *Happy Gilmore* (1996). Starring Adam Sandler, this movie is about a guy who always wanted to be a professional hockey player but then discovers he might have a talent for a different sport. He enters a golf tournament to try to win enough money to save his grandmother from losing her home to the IRS. Happy becomes an unlikely golf hero, much to the chagrin of the well-mannered golf professionals. One famous scene from the movie is a fight between Happy and Bob Barker (playing himself). Great fun!

1. *Caddyshack* (1980). Starring Bill Murry, Chevy Chase, and Rodney Dangerfield, this movie features a down-on-his-luck teen who works as a caddie at a snobby country club to raise money for his college tuition. It's a hilarious movie that is lots of fun.

Empire lists eight of these same movies in their top ten golf movies, leaving out *Caddyshack II* and *A Gentleman's Game*. In fact, they note that one reviewer called *Caddyshack II* the "worst sequel ever made, but still fun." They include instead *Tommy's Honour* (2016) and *The Caddy* (1953), a Dean Martin and Jerry Lewis comedy.

T. J. Auclair with PGA.com listed the five best golf movies, which were all in the top six of Golficity, indicating a great consensus.

CLOSING THOUGHTS

I hope this book has allowed you to adapt some of my suggested techniques to improve your golf game. In addition, these techniques perhaps will improve your life in general as you learn to become calmer and more relaxed. For some of you, a session or two with a sports psychologist might provide additional value. While there are not a ton of sports psychologists available, the field is growing. A number of psychology departments in universities now have specific training in sports psychology, making more individuals with such training available in practice. The American Psychological Association has a membership division (Division 47: Sports and Exercise Psychology), and the Association for Applied Sports Psychology has more than 1,500 members, as I mentioned in the introduction.

The number of professionals trained in sports hypnosis is even smaller, but we do exist. For information about possible referrals, you might check for referral sources through the American Society of Clinical Hypnosis. Let the site know what you are seeking, and see if there is anyone in your area. If you are a professional making money in the sport, you probably wouldn't mind traveling or paying a professional to travel to you. Further, in this day of telemedicine, a remote session is another possible approach (although I personally like to have at least one face-to-face session before doing sessions by Skype or some other media form).

Good luck! Enjoy the game, and remember to smile.

REFERENCES

Bowers, J., Hyeji Na, and G. Elkins. "Flow and Hypnotizability in a College Student Population." *International Journal of Clinical and Experimental Hypnosis* 66, no. 3 (2018): 331–42.

DiMeglio, S. "'08 US Open: A Great Tiger Tale." *USA Today Sports.* Tuesday, June 1, 2018.

Eason, A. *Hypnosis for Running: Training Your Mind to Maximise Your Running Performance.* Awake Media, 2013.

Edgette, J. H. and Rowan, T. *Winning the mind game: using hypnosis in sport psychology.* Carmathen, U.K.: Crown House Publishing, 2003.

Elkins, G. E., A. F. Barabasz, J. R. Council, and D. Spiegel. "Advancing Research and Practice: The Revised APA Division 30 Definition of Hypnosis." *International Journal of Clinical and Experimental Hypnosis* 63, no. 1 (2015): 1–9.

Ewin, D. M. "Ideomotor Signaling in the Treatment of Psychosomatic Illness." Workshop sponsored by the New Orleans Society for Clinical Hypnosis. New Orleans, LA. 2008.

Ewin, D. M., and B. N. Eimer. *Ideomotor Signals for Rapid Hypnoanalysis: A How-To Manual.* Springfield, IL: Charles Thomas Publishing, 2006.

Gallwey, W. T. *The Inner Game of Golf.* New York: Random House, 1991.

Gallwey, W. T. and Kriegel, R. J. *Inner skiing.* New York: Random House, 1979.

Gallwey, W. T. *The inner game of tennis: the classic guide to the mental side of peak performance.* New York: Random House, 1974.

Gray, J. *Talking to GOATS.* New York: HarperCollins Books, 2020.

Havens, R., and C. Walters. *Hypnotherapy Scripts: A Neo-Ericksonian Approach to Persuasive Healing.* New York: Bruner/Mazel, 1989.

Hill, N. *Think and grow rich.* Meriden, CT: the Ralston Society. 1938.

Hodenfield, C. Mental edge. *Delta Shy Magazine* (August, 2009), 76-86.

Hogan, B. *Power Golf.* New York: Gallery Books, 1948.

Karch, S. *Pathology of Drug Abuse* (4th edn). Boca Raton, FL: Taylor and Francis, 2009.

King, B. J., and C. Brennan. *Pressure Is a Privilege: Lessons I've Learned from Life and the Battle of the Sexes.* St. Louis, MO: Lifetime Media, 2008.

King, P. Five questions. *Sports Illustrated.* July 15, 1996: 74-79.

Kroger, W. S., and W. D. Fezler. *Hypnosis and Behavior Modification: Imagery Conditioning.* Philadelphia, PA: J. B. Lippincott Company, 1976.

Lebeau, J., Liu, S., Sáenz-Moncaleano, C., Sanduvete-Chaves, S., Chacón-Moscoso, S., Becker, B., and Tenenbaum, G. Quiet Eye and Performance in Sport: A Meta-Analysis. *Journal of Sport and Exercise Psychology, 38(5).* (2016): 441-457.

Lesyk, J. L. *Developing sport psychology within your clinical practice: a practical guide for mental health professionals.* San Francisco, CA: Josey-Bass, 1998.

Liggett, D. R. *Sports hypnosis.* Champaign, IL: Human Kinetics, 2000.

Loehr, J. Building a career in sport psychology: my insights, my struggles, my story. Keynote address delivered at the 25th Annual Conference of the Association of Applied Sports Psychology. Providence, RI. 2010.

Loehr, J. *The new toughness training for sports: mental, emotional, physical conditioning from one of the world's premier sports psychologists.* New York: Penguin, 1995.

Look, C. "Cell by Cell: Assessing Your Body's Natural Healing Abilities." *Hypnotherapy Today* (July 1997): 1–2.

Mack, G., and D. Casstevens. *Mind Gym: An Athlete's Guide to Inner Excellence.* Chicago, IL: Contemporary Books, 2001.

Marx, J. *The Long Snapper: A Second Chance, a Super Bowl, a Lesson for Life.* New York: Harper-Collins, 2009.

Murphy, M. *Golf in the Kingdom.* Penguin Books, 1972, 1997.

Pratt, G. J. and Korn, E. R. Using hypnosis to enhance athletic performance. In B. Zilbergeld, M.G. Edelstein, and D.L. Araoz (eds), *Hypnosis: questions and answers.* New York: W.W. Norton, (1996): 337-342.

Pulos, L. and Smith, M. Sports medicine. Workshop presented at the 40th Annual Scientific Meeting of the American Society of Clinical Hypnosis, Fort Worth, TX, 1998.

Robson, D. "Why Athletes Need a 'Quiet Eye.'" *BBC Future.* June 29, 2018.

Rotella, R. *Golf Is Not a Game of Perfect.* New York: Simon and Schuster, 1995.

Rotella, R. *Golf Is a Game of Confidence.* New York: Simon and Schuster, 1996.

Rotella, R. *The Golfer's Mind.* New York: Simon and Schuster, 2004.

Rotella, R. *Your Fifteenth Club: The Inner Secret to Great Golf.* New York: Simon and Schuster, 2008.

Rotella, R., and B. Cullen. *The Unstoppable Golfer: Trusting Your Mind and Your Short Game to Achieve Greatness.* New York: Simon and Schuster, 2012.

Rotella, R. *How Champions Think: In Sports and In Life.* New York: Simon and Schuster, 2015.

Saunders, T. *Golf: The Mind-Body Connection: How to Lower Your Score with Mental Training.* Mind-Body Golf, 1996.

Saunders, T. *Golf: Lower Your Score with Mind Training.* Carmarthen, UK: Crown House Publishing, 2005.

Schwartz, D. Brains and brawn. *Monitor on Psychology,* 39(7). (2008): 54-56.

Selye, H. *The stress of life.* New York: McGraw-Hill, 1956.

Shipnuck, A. Last man standing. *Sports Illustrated,* April 2009. 30-34.

Taylor, J., Stone, K.R., Mullin, M.J., Ellenbecker, T., and Walgenbach, A. *Comprehensive Sports Injury Management: From Examination of Injury to Return to Sport.* Austin, TX: Pro-Ed, 2003.

Taylor, J. and Taylor, S. *Psychological Approaches to Sports Injury Rehabilitation.* Gaithersburg, MD: Aspen Publications, 1997.

Thompson, R. A. and Sherman R. T. *Helping Athletes with Eating Disorders: A User's Guide*. Champaign, IL: Human Kinetics, 1993.

Tramontana, J. *HEAT: hypnotically enhanced addictions treatment: an overview*. Workshop presented at the 58th Annual Convention of the Mississippi Psychological Association, Tunica, MS. 2008.

Tramontana, J. *Hypnotically Enhanced Treatment for Addictions: Alcohol Abuse, Drug Abuse, Gambling, Weight Control, and Smoking Cessation*. Carmarthen, UK: Crown House Publishing, 2009.

Tramontana, J. *Sports Hypnosis in Practice: Scripts, Strategies, and Case Examples*. Carmarthen. UK: Crown House Publishing, 2011.

Tramontana, J. Subject bias as a significant factor in hypnotic instructions with child clients. *Hypnotherapy Today*, December 1983, 1.

Tramontana, J. Successful blepharoplasty with self-hypnosis, a spousal "coach," and only local anesthesia: a case report. *Psychological Hypnosis: A Bulletin of APA Division 30*, 17, no 3. 2008, 4-7.

Van Raalte, J. L. and Brewer, B.W. (eds) *Exploring sport and exercise psychology*. Washington, D.C.: American Psychological Association, 2002.

Wadler, G.I. and Hainline, B. *Drugs and the Athlete*. Philadelphia, PA: F.A. Davis Company, 1989.

Wark, D. From the president's desk. *American Society of Clinical Hypnosis Newsletter*, Fall (2008): 1.

Williams, J. M., and Leffingwell, T. R. *Cognitive strategies in sport and exercise psychology*. Washington, D.C.: American Psychological Association, (2002), 75-98.

Yapko, M. D. *Trancework: An Introduction to the Practice of Clinical Hypnosis*. New York: Routledge Publishing, 2012.

CPSIA information can be obtained
at www.ICGtesting.com
Printed in the USA
BVHW081538310521
608479BV00002B/251